MW00963212

MISSISSIPPI

THE NEW ILLUSTRATED GUIDE TO THE

MODERN
US NAVY

THE NEW ILLUSTRATED GUIDE TO THE

MODERN
US NAVY

JOHN JORDAN

A Salamander Book

©1992 Salamander Books Ltd.,
129-137 York Way,
London N7 9LG,
United Kingdom.

ISBN 0 8317-5061-8

This edition published in 1992 by
SMITHMARK Publishers, Inc.,
16 East 32nd Street, New York,
NY 10016.

SMITHMARK Books are available for
bulk purchase for sales promotion
and premium use. For details write or
call the Manager of Special Sales,
SMITHMARK Publishers, Inc.,
16 East 32nd Street, New York, NY
10016. (212) 532-6600.

Credits

Author: John Jordan is a contributor
to many important defence journals,
a consultant to the Soviet section of
"Jane's Fighting Ships" and co-author
of Salamander's "Balance of Military
Power".

Editor: Chris Westhorp
Designers: Mark Holt & Tim Scott

Photographs: All official US Navy
photographs supplied by Navy
Department, US Department of
Defense, Washington, DC.
Line drawings: ©John Jordan.
Filmset by The Old Mill, London.
Color reproduction by Scantrans
PTE, Singapore.
Printed in Hong Kong

Cover: DDG 51 *Arleigh Burke* by Stephen Seymour, ©Salamander Books Ltd.
Below: Operating from USS *Deyo*, a SH-60B LAMPS MK3 helicopter
       conducts an ASW patrol for the battle group.

Contents

Vessels are arranged within sections of classes, and are listed under the name ship of that class. Classification initials begin each entry and are explained on page 9.

Introduction
Development of the US Navy 6
Aircraft Carriers
Nimitz 16
Kitty Hawk 22
Enterprise 28
Forrestal 32
Submarines
Ohio 36
Lafayette 40
Seawolf 42
Los Angeles 44
Sturgeon 48
Cruisers
Ticonderoga 50
Virginia 56
California 60
Belknap 62
Bainbridge 66
Leahy 68
Long Beach 72
Destroyers
Arleigh Burke 74
Kidd 78
Spruance 80
Frigates
Oliver Hazard Perry 86
Knox 92
Patrol Combatants
Pegasus 96

Osprey 98
Avenger 100
Amphibious Warfare Vessels
Blue Ridge 102
Wasp 104
Tarawa 108
Iwo Jima 114
Austin 118
Raleigh 120
Whidbey Island 122
Anchorage 124
Newport 126
Support Ships
Yellowstone/Gompers 128
E.S. Land/L.Y. Spear 130
Simon Lake/Hunley 132
Replenishment Ships
Kilauea 134
Suribachi 136
Mars 138
Cimarron 140
Supply 142
Sacramento 144
Wichita 146
Weapons and Sensors
Aircraft 148
Surveillance Radars 152
Air-Defence 154
Anti-Submarine 156
Anti-Surface 158

Development of the US Navy

The geographical situation of the United States, separated from Europe by the Atlantic and from the mainland of Asia by the even broader expanses of the Pacific, makes the possession of a strong navy imperative. The United States Navy is the primary instrument for the projection of American military power and political influence into these distant regions, and it is at the same time the means by which the United States maintains control over the seas in order to ensure the security of its maritime communications and of its territory in the event of hostilities with another power.

These twin missions of power projection and sea control cannot be considered in total isolation from one another. In order to project power against a distant land mass a navy must be able to exercise control over the seas which its forces will have to transit in order to reach their objective and over the operating area from which the air strikes and amphibious assault will be made. Similarly, the job of exercising sea control over broad ocean areas is

made much easier if forward-deployed power projection forces compel the enemy to adopt a defensive posture. The power projection and sea control missions should therefore be seen as two sides of the same coin. The problem is that of finding the right balance between those forces required for "offensive" — ie, power projection — missions and those required for "defensive" — ie, sea control — missions.

In time of war, when funds and resources are virtually unlimited, there is no conflict of interests; a country the size of the United States simply builds what it needs. In peacetime, however, the inevitable constraints on the defence budget mean that difficult choices have to be made; more of one type of ship means less of another. Factions supporting a particular aspect of naval operations — the aviators, the submarines, the surface ship lobby — begin to dig their heels in, and bitter

conflicts break out over the crucial issue of what sort of forces the navy should have, and in what numbers. It is against this background that the development of the US Navy over the past three decades must be seen.

The Postwar Era
In the years which followed World War II Western naval thinking was dominated by two factors: the advent of the atomic bomb, and the acquisition of German submarine technology by the Soviet Navy.

The atomic bomb threatened traditional naval task forces based on aircraft-carriers and amphibious assault ships, which constituted the primary means by which the Western nations could project their military power. The creation by the Soviet Navy of a large force of advanced commerce-raiding submarines threatened the lines of communication between the countries of the NATO Alliance, which unlike those of the Soviet Union and its allies were dependent on merchant ships, not trains, to transport troops, tanks, and munitions to the Central Front.

The US Navy's response to these twin threats was to construct a series of "super-carriers" capable of operating large bombers which could make long-range nuclear strikes on Soviet territory. These carriers would be protected by powerful jet fighter aircraft vectored out in the direction of hostile air attack under the control of airborne early warning aircraft. The new carriers would ensure the continued viability of the sea-based power projection mission.

The anti-submarine problem was tackled in a different way. The US Navy ended World War II with a large force of medium-sized fleet carriers and vast numbers of conventional destroyers armed with guns and torpedoes. During the 1950s 12 of those carriers were re-designated Anti-submarine Support Carriers (CVS) and allocated a revised air group comprising S-2 Tracker ASW aircraft and HSS-1 helicopters. They

Left: The carrier battle groups continue to be the primary means by which the United States projects its military power.

Above: *Dwight D. Eisenhower* (CVN 69) transits northbound through the Suez Canal in Egypt in August 1990 bound for the Mediterranean Sea. Over the next few months dozens of well-armed warships were to head in the opposite direction en route to the Arabian Gulf.

would become the focus of submarine hunter-killer groups and convoy escort groups. Subsequently, in the early 1960s, large numbers of the war-built destroyers underwent FRAM (Fleet Rehabilitation and Modernisation) refits to equip them with new sonars and modern anti-submarine weapons.

Zumwalt and the Sea Control Programme

The traditional convoy strategy was a viable counter to the perceived Soviet anti-submarine threat as long as there were sufficient escorts avail

able. However, by the early 1970s the ASW support carriers and the war-built destroyers were 25 years old and the US Navy was facing the problem of "block obsolescence".

Admiral Zumwalt, the new Chief of Naval Operations (CNO), inherited a naval programme comprising exclusively high-performance task force vessels designed for the power projection mission: the Nimitz class CVANs, the Tarawa class LHAs, the Virginia class CGNs, the Spruance class DDs and the Los Angeles class SSNs (all three of the last-named types designed to operate with the

US NAVY CLASSIFICATION SYSTEM

CVN	nuclear-powered aircraft carrier	MCM	mine counter-measures
		LCC	amphibious command ship
CV	aircraft carrier	LHD/LHA	amphibious assault ship (multi-purpose)
SSBN	nuclear-powered ballistic submarine	LPH	amphibious assault ship
SSN	nuclear-powered attack submarine	LPD	amphibious transport dock
CG	missile cruiser	LSD	dock landing ship
CGN	nuclear-powered missile cruiser	LST	tank landing ship
		AD	destroyer tender
DDG	missile destroyer (AAW)	AS	submarine tender
DD	destroyer (ASW)	AE	ammunition ship
FFG	missile frigate (AAW)	AFS	combat support ship
FF	frigate (ASW)	AO	oiler
PHM	missile patrol hydrofoil	AOE	fast combat support ship
MHC	coastal minehunter	AOR	replenishment oiler

carrier battle groups).

Zumwalt proposed to complement these "gold-plated" warships with a programme of inexpensive vessels of moderate performance which could be produced in large numbers for the sea control mission. Within 60 days of his accession he produced Project 60, which was to form the basis of the US Navy's construction programme of the 1970s.

The "high" element of this "High/Low" programme was already in place, and the only modification possible was the cancellation of the last four LHAs. The "low" programme therefore had to be financed largely by the premature retirement of large numbers of war-built ships. It focused on four new classes, the most important of which were the Patrol Frigate (PF) and the Sea Control Ship (SCS).

The Patrol Frigate (which became the Oliver Hazard Perry class) was a development of the convoy escort types built during the 1960s, but with enhanced AAW and anti-surface capabilities in order to counter the new Soviet long-range maritime bombers and forward-deployed surface units. The Sea Control Ship was an austere ASW carrier capable of operating 14 SH-3 Sea King ASW helicopters and three AV-8A Harrier aircraft. Eight could be purchased for the price of a single CVAN.

Zumwalt was concerned about the vulnerability of the US Navy's super-carriers to pre-emptive attack by Soviet surface action groups armed with anti-ship missiles, and wanted an end to the forward deployment of these ships. He proposed that the more expendable Sea Control Ships should replace them in forward areas such as the eastern Mediterranean. The super-carriers would be held back in low-threat areas until the outbreak of hostilities, when they would exchange places with the SCS. Surface warships would be fitted with anti-ship missiles, which would effectively distribute strike power between a multitude of hulls, thereby making a Soviet pre-emptive strike prohibitively difficult.

This was heresy to the power projection lobby, which feared a cut-off of funds for new carrier construction and carrier aviation programmes, and the policies instigated by Zumwalt were put into reverse shortly after his retirement from the post of CNO in 1974. The escort programme survived but the SCS, which was central to the philosophy, did not.

Moreover the very concept of low-value, low-performance ships which formed the basis of the sea control programme came under increasing attack. There were many who felt that rather than trying to "hold the line" against the Soviet Navy with dwindling numbers of escort ships, the US Navy should go onto the offensive and make its undoubted technological superiority count. Such a policy would require high-value, high-performance ships capable of operating in high-threat areas. The result was the Aegis cruiser, with

their sophisticated radar and missile systems for task force air-defence, and a renewal of the super-carrier construction programme.

New ASW Technology

By the late 1970s there was increasing confidence that new technology would in any case make large numbers of convoy escort vessels an expensive anachronism.

Since the early 1960s the US Navy had been constructing an extensive network of passive acoustic sensors located in fixed strategic positions on the seabed around the North Atlantic and the Pacific. Advances made in micro-processor technology during the early 1970s would bring quantum improvements in data analysis, enabling the US Navy to locate and track most of the Soviet submarines deployed in these waters to within about 50nm of their true position.

P-3C Orion "pouncer" aircraft, equipped with sophisticated sensors, were to be dispatched from airfields in North America and Iceland in order to localise the contact, and in the event of hostilities would attempt to sink the submarine with ASW homing torpedoes or depth bombs. The US Navy's Orions would be complemented in the eastern Atlantic and Norwegian/North Sea areas by European maritime patrol aircraft; British Nimrods, Dutch and Norwegian Orions, and German Atlantics. Cover for the mid-Atlantic area could be provided from the decks of the super-carriers, which now carried a squadron of 10 S-3 Viking fixed-wing aircraft capable of acquiring and prosecuting a submarine contact 250nm (460km) or more from the carrier battle group.

Further developments included linear passive arrays towed by surface vessels and submarines. Those

currently fitted aboard frigates and SSNs generally have detection ranges equivalent to two "convergence zones" (ie, about 70nm or 130km), while larger arrays now coming into service aboard purpose-built outsize tugs designated T-AGOS can cover much broader ocean areas.

These broad-area detection systems were seen as being of greatest value in the period immediately preceding hostilities, as they would enable the West to locate most of the Soviet submarines already in the North Atlantic. However, it was feared that these systems might quickly be degraded once a conflict began, and it would then be necessary to institute other anti-submarine strategies in order to protect transatlantic shipping. The decline of the Western merchant fleets was such that they no longer had the capacity to sustain the losses which had been acceptable in World War II, and the possibility of a protracted conventional conflict in which industrial capacity would again play an important part made their protection all the more important.

The NATO answer to the shortage of escorts was to opt for the creation of anti-submarine "barriers" through which Soviet submarines would have to pass in order to reach the shipping lanes. In the North Atlantic area the first of these barriers, designed to intercept Soviet submarines as they sortied from their bases in the Barents Sea, ran in a northerly direction from just west of the North Cape of Norway. The proximity of this barrier to Soviet bases necessarily restricted its composition to maritime patrol aircraft and hunter-killer submarines. However, the main barrier, which in addition was to comprise anti-submarine minefields and major surface warships operating ASW helicopters, was to be in what is known as the Greenland/Iceland/United Kingdom (GIUK) Gap. The primary function of this barrier was to stop Soviet sub-

marines breaking out into the open spaces of the North Atlantic.

Soviet submarines which escaped the net would continue to be a problem, as there would be sufficient escorts only for major military convoys, and other shipping might have to sail independently. Until the 1980s it was envisaged that the bulk of the US Pacific Fleet would have to be shifted to the Atlantic at the outbreak of hostilities in order to boost both the striking forces and the number of escorts available in that area, thereby effectively precluding any major offensive operations against the Soviet Navy in the north-west Pacific Ocean.

The Maritime Strategy

The primary aim of the Maritime Strategy, which became the basis for US naval thinking during the early 1980s, was to shift the focus from potential allied sea control weaknesses to utilising US Navy power projection capabilities to put pressure on the Soviet Navy, thereby compelling the Soviets to adopt a defensive posture.

The fundamental principles of the strategy were: aggressive forward deployment in peacetime, in order to control crises in the Third World areas where they were most likely to develop, and prevent escalation; and the need to seize an early initiative in fighting, which would be achieved by the rapid deployment of all available power projection forces in the period immediately preceding the outbreak of hostilities. The strategy of forward defence was based on seeking out the Soviet Navy in its

Below: Adoption of the Maritime Strategy in the 1980s implied large numbers of expensive, sophisticated surface combatants, such as the Aegis cruisers of the Ticonderoga class, which would be considered well-capable of operations in high-threat areas.

most likely areas of deployment (ie, off northern Norway and in the north-west Pacific) and systematically destroying both its ships and its operational bases. An important aspect of forward defence was that it would be seen to guarantee early support to the United States' West European NATO allies, and would encourage the active participation of those countries in an aggressive containment strategy.

The Soviet Navy would not be able to sit back and defend its corner, but would be drawn into a desperate defence of Soviet sea-space against US Navy offensive operations on every flank. In a fundamental change of deployment posture, the US Pacific Fleet would no longer be withdrawn through the Panama Canal to bolster western sea control operations in the North Atlantic area, but would conduct a vigorous offensive against Soviet ships and bases in the north-west Pacific. Western nuclear-powered attack submarines (SSNs) would be deployed in support of the carrier battle groups, and would be used to infiltrate the Soviet bastions, where they would hunt down Soviet SSBNs and launch precision-guided Tomahawk land-attack missiles against Soviet military targets on the Kola Peninsula and the Siberian mainland.

The effect on NATO anti-submarine operations in the North Atlantic would be to reduce the pressure on the barriers and the military convoys by deflecting the attentions of Soviet attack submarines, which would have to be deployed defensively to protect their own forces in the bastion areas.

The Maritime Strategy was not without its critics, many of whom were concerned about the threat of strategic destabilisation implicit in the proposed assault on the Soviet SSBN bastions. However, it was generally welcomed by the US Navy, which was never comfortable with the essentially defensive "Atlantic" strategy which preceded it.

The new strategy was to be underpinned by the construction of new super-carriers, which would replace the ageing Forrestals completed during the mid-1950s; an extended construction programme for the Aegis cruiser, which would provide sophisticated air-defence in high-threat areas; and authorization of a new type of fleet destroyer, the DDG 51, which would complement the Aegis cruisers in the carrier battle groups.

There would also be a new type of nuclear-powered attack submarine, the Seawolf, designed specifically to operate within the bastion areas. A pump-jet propulsion system would ensure an exceptionally high "quiet" speed, and the Seawolf would be much larger than previous types of SSN to enable it to accommodate twice as many torpedoes and missiles. The increase in payload would enable these boats to operate for longer periods in the target-rich environment offered by the bastions, and would therefore reduce the need for frequent runs through the bastion boundary defences in order to replenish.

The "New World Order"

The Maritime Strategy was essentially a response to the Soviet threat. When this threat crumbled in the late 1980s as a result of the internal reforms and foreign policy initiatives of President Mikhail Gorbachev, many of the key assumptions of the Maritime Strategy were invalidated, and it was quietly abandoned. The policy now evolving lays the emphasis on sustaining and supporting US political and economic interests around the world by a rapid intervention capability. On 2 August 1990 — ironically the day of the Iraqi invasion of Kuwait — President Bush defined the four major elements of the new US defence policy as: forward presence; crisis response; force reconstitution; and deterrence.

In February of the following year the US Chief of Naval Operations, Frank B. Kelso II, argued that only maritime superiority could effectively underpin these four elements. He further stated that the key components of the new naval policy are as follows: surge forces for rapid deployment to any crisis; forward-deployed expeditionary forces with full logistics support capable of going anywhere; a sea-based maritime pre-positioned force; and sea-based strategic forces for deterrence.

Although not stated officially, it has become clear that power projection has now replaced ASW as the Navy's top war-fighting priority. Not only has the 600-ship goal of the early 1980s been abandoned, but the majority of the ships which will decommission over the next few years will be ocean escorts of the Knox and Oliver Hazard Perry classes. Response to regional conflict will require *local* sea control only, while the decreased likelihood of conflict with the Soviet Union increases strategic warning time, allowing 25 per cent of surface ASW forces to be placed in reserve, for activation in 180 days. The Seawolf submarine programme has also been reduced to a single unit, in part because of rocketing costs but also because of its lack of relevance to future defence requirements as they are currently perceived.

There will be a reduction to either 10 or 12 operational carriers, but it has been stated that the carrier battle group (CVBG) will remain the primary force for power projection and the centrepiece of a balanced fleet. The major problem for the carrier fleet, in the wake of the cancellation of the key A-12 attack aircraft programme, will be the provision of high-performance aircraft in sufficient numbers to sustain the quality of the air wings. Similar problems face the Marine amphibious forces, whose ability to execute effective over-the-horizon airborne assaults was dependent on the MV-22 Osprey tilt-rotor aircraft, funding for which is being denied by the US Department of Defense against substantial congressional opposition.

Overall numbers of ships will decline to 451 in Financial Year (FY) 1995, making it possible to forward-deploy two/three carriers, 25-30 surface combatants, 14 SSNs, and two/three amphibious ready groups for presence or crisis response. These deployments represent 30 per cent of total forces and could be sustained indefinitely, with additional units being "surged" in the event of imminent hostilities.

Below: The need for large, costly SSNs is increasingly being questioned now that the Soviet threat has given way to potential operations against less formidable shallow-water navies.

Aircraft Carriers

CVN
Nimitz

Completed:	1975 onwards.
Names:	CVN 68 *Nimitz*; CVN 69 *Dwight D. Eisenhower*; CVN 70 *Carl Vinson*; CVN 71 *Theodore Roosevelt*; CVN 72 *Abraham Lincoln*; CVN 73 *George Washington* †; CVN 74 *John C. Stennis* †; CVN 75 *United States* †. (†building)
Displacement:	81,600t standard; 93,300 full load.*
Dimensions:	Length 1,092ft oa (332.8m); beam 134ft wl (40.8m); 251ft flight deck (76.4m); draught 37ft (11.3m).*
Propulsion:	Four-shaft nuclear; two A4W reactors driving geared steam turbines; 260,000shp = 30kts.
Armament:	Three Sea Sparrow launchers Mk 29 (3x8); three/four Mk 15 Phalanx CIWS.
Aircraft:	20 F-14A Tomcat; 20 F/A-18 Hornet; 16 A-6E Intruder; five EA-6B Prowler; five E-2C Hawkeye; eight S-3A/B Viking; six SH-3G/H Sea King or SH-60F Seahawk.
Sensors:	*Surveillance*: SPS-48C/E, SPS-49, SPS-67. *Fire-Control*: Three Mk91

(*Figures for CVN 68/69. Later units have greater displacement/draught.)

The Nimitz class was originally envisaged as a replacement for the three Midway class carriers. The completion of the first nuclear-powered carrier, *Enterprise*, had been followed by the construction of two conventionally powered ships, *America* and *John F. Kennedy*. The latter had, however, only ever been thought of as "interim" designs to plug the gap between *Enterprise* and a second generation of nuclear carriers which would employ smaller numbers of more advanced reactors to provide the necessary power, and which would, it was hoped, cost less to build. The two A4W reactors which power the Nimitz class each produce approximately 130,000shp compared with only 35,000shp for each of the eight A2W reactors aboard *Enterprise*. Moreover, the uranium cores need replacing far less frequently than those originally used in *Enterprise*, giving a full 13-year period between refuellings.

Below: *Carl Vinson* (CVN 70), with a deck-load of F-14 fleet air-defence fighters and attack aircraft. Note the two Phalanx CIWS at the stern.

Above: *Nimitz* (CVN 68). Rows of A-6 Intruders and EA-6B Prowlers are lined up on the starboard edge of the expansive flight deck.

Below: The Nimitz class has the now-standard US Navy flight deck layout, with four deck-edge lifts, three of them to starboard.

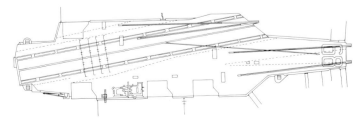

The reduction in the number of reactors from eight to two allowed for major improvements in the internal arrangements below hangar-deck level. Whereas in *Enterprise* the entire centre section of the ship is occupied by the machinery rooms, with the aviation fuel compartments and munitions magazines pushed out towards the ends of the ship, in *Nimitz* the propulsion machinery is divided into two separate units, with the magazines between them and forward of them. The improved arrangement has resulted in an increase of 20 per cent in aviation fuel capacity and a similar increase in the volume available for munitions and general stores.

The decks and hull have been constructed of extra-strong high-tensile steel to limit the impact of armour-piercing bombs. Subdivision is exceptionally thorough, with 23 watertight transverse bulkheads, and firefighting facilities are sophisticated and comprehensive. Later units of the class have 6.35cm (2.5in) of Kevlar armour over certain areas of the side shell, and there is box protection for magazine and machinery spaces which is being retro-fitted to earlier ships.

The flight deck layout is virtually identical to that of *John F. Kennedy* (CV 67). The angled deck is 800ft (238m) long, and there are four Mk 7 arrestor wires and four C13-1 catapults. Each of the four aircraft lifts measures 70ft by 52ft (21.3m x 15.8m) and has a capacity of 47 tons. At hangar deck level there has been a significant increase in the provision of maintenance workshops and spare parts stowage, and there is a large bay aft for aero-engine maintenance and testing. The complement, including aircrew, is almost 6,300 men (the original Forrestal design, on which all US super-carriers are based, provided for only 3,800!).

As completed the first three ships had an SPS-48C 3-D radar atop the island superstructure and an SPS-43A long-range air surveillance radar on a lattice mast abaft the island. The latter was replaced by SPS-49 during the mid-1980s,

Below: An early view of *Dwight D. Eisenhower* (CVN 69), with A-7 Corsair and A-6 Intruder attack aircraft amidships, F-14 Tomcat fleet air-defence fighters aft and several E-2C Hawkeye to starboard.

and the SPS-48C is due to be replaced by SPS-48E, which has double the effective radiated power.

Nimitz and *Eisenhower* were initially armed with three Mk 25 BPDMS missile systems with optical sights. The third ship, *Carl Vinson*, which entered service in 1982, was fitted from the outset with three Mk 29 launchers for Sea Sparrow, with Mk 91 radar fire-control, plus four Mk 15 Phalanx CIWS. These systems were subsequently retro-fitted to the first two ships, which however received only three Phalanx CIWS. All have now received the Mk 23 TAS target designation system, which is designed to provide rapid acquisition of low-flying aircraft and anti-ship missiles.

A full Naval Tactical Data System (NTDS) is installed. During the mid-1980s the first three ships were fitted with an Anti-Submarine Classification and Analysis Center (ASCAC), which permits instant sharing of data between the carrier, its ASW aircraft, and task force escorts. Later units have been completed with both NTDS and the ASCAC.

Authorization of the fourth ship was delayed by concerns regarding cost, the Carter Administration favouring first the 60,000 ton CVV, a smaller, less capable

Left: A modernised Forrestal class carrier cruising in the hostile waters of the Gulf during the war with Iraq. Note the standard sponson for Sea Sparrow, and the SPS-49 air search radar.

Below: A Sea Sparrow missile is launched from *Dwight D. Eisenhower* (CVN 69). US Navy carriers rely principally on their force of better-armed battle group escorts for area air-defence.

design, and then a conventionally-powered repeat of the *John F. Kennedy*. CVN 71 was finally authorized in 1980, and became the first of a new series; two further ships were authorized in 1983, and two more in 1988. Five units of the class are now in service with a sixth, *George Washington*, due for completion in mid-1992; CVN 69 and 71 are in the Atlantic, and the other three in the Pacific. Later ships will replace the Forrestal class in service.

Below: The brightly-lit operations room in a carrier of the Nimitz class. These ships now have an ASCAC as well as NTDS.

Kitty Hawk

Completed: 1961-8.
Names: CV 63 *Kitty Hawk*; CV 64 *Constellation*; CV 66 *America*; CV 67 *John F. Kennedy*.
Displacement: 60,100t light; 81,775t full load.*
Dimensions: Length 1,062ft oa (323.6m); beam 130ft wl (39.6m); 252ft flight deck (76.8m); draught 37ft (11.4m).*
Propulsion: Four-shaft geared steam turbines; 280,000shp = 30kts.
Armament: Three Sea Sparrow launchers Mk 29 (3 × 8); three Phalanx Mk 15 CIWS.
Aircraft: 20 F-14A Tomcat; 20 F/A-18 Hornet; 16 A-6E Intruder; five EA-6B Prowler; five E-2C Hawkeye; eight S-3A/B Viking; six SH-3G/H Sea King or SH-60F Seahawk.
Sensors: *Surveillance*; SPS-48C/E, SPS-49, SPS-10F or SPS-67. *Fire-Control*: Three Mk91
(*Figures for *Kitty Hawk* (CV 63). *John F. Kennedy* is slightly larger.)

Although there are significant differences between the first pair completed and the last two vessels — *John F. Kennedy* (CV 67) is officially considered as a separate single-ship class — these four carriers are generally grouped together because of their common propulsion system and flight deck layout.

Left and above: Two views of *Kitty Hawk* (CV 63), now rearmed with three Sea Sparrow launchers and three Phalanx CIWS. The aircraft in the foreground are A-7 Corsairs, now mostly replaced by F/A-18s.

Above: F-14A Tomcat fleet air-defence fighters aboard *John F. Kennedy* (CV 67) during operations in the Red Sea in late 1990. The wings are fully swept for economical deck stowage. The two aircraft at top left are SA-3A Vikings; the helicopters at bottom left are SH-3H Sea Kings. The make-up of the carrier's air wing is currently in transition.

Kitty Hawk (CV 63) and *Constellation* (CV 64) were ordered as improved Forrestals, incorporating a number of important modifications. The flight deck showed a slight increase in area, and the arrangement of the lifts was revised to improve aircraft-handling arrangements. The single port-side lift, which on the Forrestals was located at the forward end of the flight deck — and was therefore unusable during landing operations — was repositioned at the after end of the overhang, outside the line of the angled deck. The respective positions of the centre lift on the starboard side and the island structure were reversed, so that two lifts were available to serve the forward catapults. A further improved feature of the lifts was that they were no longer strictly rectangular, but had an additional angled section at their forward end which enabled longer aircraft to be accommodated. The new arrangement proved so successful that it was adopted by all subsequent US carriers.

America (CV 66), the third ship of the class, was completed after a gap of four years and incorporated a number of further modifications. She has a narrower funnel and she was initially fitted with an SQS-23 sonar (removed in 1981).

As completed these three ships were fitted with two Terrier SAM systems, the Mk 10 launchers being positioned on sponsons aft just beneath the level of the flight deck. The need to accommodate SPG-55 fire-control radars, together with a full outfit of surveillance and height-finding radars, led to the adoption of a separate lattice mast stepped abaft the island. This has carried a succession of large 3-D radars, culminating in the planar SPS-48.

The Terrier SAM system proved expensive in terms of both cost and space, and merely duplicated capabilities already available on carrier escorts. It was therefore abandoned in the fourth ship, *John F. Kennedy* (CV 67), which was fitted only with three Mk 25 launchers for the Basic Point Defense Missile System (BPDMS). Further modifications included a distinctive canted funnel, and a slightly modified flight deck layout, which was to be adopted for all subsequent US super-carriers. Provision was made, as in *America*, for the SQS-23 sonar, but this was never installed.

All four ships were subsequently brought up to a similar standard. The Terrier systems were removed around 1980 and replaced by Mk 29 Sea Sparrow launchers (initially two, then three) and Mk 15 Phalanx CIWS. Radar systems were standardized around the SPS-48 3-D radar and the SPS-43A long-range air surveillance radar (subsequently replaced by SPS-49). During the 1980s all received the ASCAC anti-submarine tactical data system and Mk 23 TAS.

From 1988-91 *Kitty Hawk* (CV 63) underwent a major refit at Philadelphia as part of the Service Life Extension Program (SLEP). SLEP, which aims to extend the life of a carrier by 15 years, involves a complete overhaul of propulsion and auxiliary machinery, the renewal of pipework, and upgrading of weapons and electronics systems. In *Kitty Hawk* the SPS-48C radar has been replaced by SPS-48E, Mk 23 TAS has been fitted, and the NTDS and electronic warfare suite have been upgraded. She can now handle the SH-60F Sea Hawk, which is replacing the SH-3 Sea King. *Constellation* (CV 64) is now undergoing a similar

refit, which will be completed in 1993. Following the decision to reduce the number of operational carrier battle groups, SLEP refits will be abandoned, and *John F. Kennedy* (CV 67), which was due to enter SLEP in 1992, will now receive only a "complex overhaul".

Kitty Hawk (CV 63), *America* (CV 66) and *John F. Kennedy* (CV 67) all serve in the Atlantic. *Constellation* (CV 64) will rejoin the Pacific Fleet on completion of her SLEP refit in 1993.

Below: *John F. Kennedy* (CV 67) takes on fuel and dry stores from a fast combat support ship of the Sacramento class. The vessel to starboard is a Ticonderoga class cruiser. Note the distinctive canted stack of the 'JFK', not to mention the deck space available.

CVN

Enterprise

Completed: 1961.
Name: CVN 65 *Enterprise*.
Displacement: 75,700t standard; 93,970t full load.
Dimensions: Length 1,123ft oa (342.3m); beam 133ft wl (40.5m); 248ft flight deck (75.7m); draught 39ft (11.9m).
Propulsion: Four-shaft nuclear; eight A2W reactors driving geared steam turbines; 280,000shp = 30kts.
Armament: Three Sea Sparrow launchers Mk 29 (3 × 8); three Mk 15 Phalanx CIWS.
Aircraft: 20 F-14A Tomcat; 20 F/A-18 Hornet; 16 A-6E Intruder; five EA-6B Prowler; five E-2C Hawkeye; eight S-3A/B Viking; six SH-60F Seahawk.
Sensors: *Surveillance*: SPS-48E, SPS-49, SPS-67.
Fire-Control: Three Mk91

Laid down shortly after the US Navy's first nuclear-powered surface ship, the cruiser *Long Beach*, *Enterprise* (CVN 65) was completed in the remarkably short space of three years nine months. The initial development work on her propulsion plant had begun as early as 1950, and the design of the reactors had benefited from the evaluation of early models installed in submarines. Even so, the problem of producing the required 280,000shp on four shafts employing first-generation reactors resulted in a solution that was costly in terms of internal volume: two A2W reactors are coupled to each shaft and the entire centre section of the ship is taken up by machinery.

Enterprise was also costly in monetary terms — nearly double that of her conventionally-powered contemporaries of the Kitty Hawk class — but a number of strong arguments were advanced in favour of nuclear power. Reduced life-cycle costs due to infrequent refuellings made the nuclear-powered carrier a

Below: *Enterprise* (CVN 65) following her major refit, in which the original SPS-32/33 "billboard" radars were removed and replaced by conventional rotating antennae. She is now fitted out with Sea Sparrow and the Mk 15 Phalanx Close-In Weapons System.

more economic proposition in the longer term, and the CVAN would be capable of undertaking lengthy transits and operations in high-threat areas at a high sustained speed. Moreover, the elimination of ship's fuel bunkers in *Enterprise* allowed a 50 per cent increase in aviation fuel capacity, and consequently in the number of consecutive days of strike operations she could sustain.

In size and general layout *Enterprise* is similar to *Kitty Hawk*. The most significant difference as completed was in the shape of the island, which comprised a "box" structure on which were mounted SPS-32/33 "billboard" radars, surmounted by a large cone for ECM and ESM antennae. The SPS-32/33 radars proved difficult to maintain, however, and when *Enterprise* was refitted in 1979-81 they were removed and replaced by conventional rotating antennae of the latest types located atop the island.

Like the carriers of the Kitty Hawk class *Enterprise* was to have received two Mk 10 launchers for Terrier missiles. She was completed with the large sponsons

aft, but Terrier was not installed initially in a bid to keep down costs. When Terrier lost favour as a carrier weapon in the mid-1960s, it was decided instead to fit two BPDMS Sea Sparrow launchers on the after sponsons. At her 1979-81 refit these were replaced by Mk 29 launchers for Sea Sparrow, with Mk 91 radar fire-control, and she received three Mk 15 Phalanx CIWS.

During her current refit, due to last until 1994, *Enterprise* will receive a third Mk 29 launcher, Mk 23 TAS, and the advanced SPS-48E radar. NTDS and the ASCAC ASW data analysis centre are already fitted, and these will be complemented by a Tactical Flag Command Center (TFCC). Having served in the Pacific theatre throughout the 1970s and 1980s, *Enterprise* was transferred to the Atlantic Fleet in 1989.

Below: *Enterprise* at speed. Nuclear propulsion translates into the ability to deploy rapidly over long distances without the need for refuelling.

CV
Forrestal

Completed: 1952-55.
Names: CV 59 *Forrestal*; CV 60 *Saratoga*; CV 61 *Ranger*, CV 62 *Independence*.
Displacement: 60,000t light; 79,250t full load.*
Dimensions: Length 1,085ft oa (331m); beam 132ft wl (39.6m); 250ft flight deck (76.3m); draught 37ft (11.3m).*
Propulsion: Four-shaft geared steam turbines; 260-280,000shp = 33kts.
Armament: Two /three Sea Sparrow launchers Mk 29 (2/3 × 8); three Mk 15 Phalanx CIWS.
Aircraft: 20 F-14A Tomcat; 20 F/A-18 Hornet; 16 A-6E Intruder; five EA-6B Prowler; five E-2C Hawkeye; eight S-3A/B Viking; six SH-3G/H Sea King or SH-60F Seahawk.
Sensors: *Surveillance:* SPS-48C, SPS-49, SPS-67. *Fire-Control:* Two/three Mk 91.

(*Figures for *Forrestal* (CV 59).)

Authorisation of the Forrestal class was a direct consequence of the Korean War, which re-established the value of the carrier for projecting air power against land targets. The new class was to operate the A-3 Skywarrior strategic bomber, which weighed fully 78,000lb (35,455kg) and dimensions and hangar height were increased accordingly. The original design was for a carrier similar in configuration to the ill-fated *United States*, which had a flush deck, together with a retractable bridge, and two waist catapults angled out on sponsons in addition to the standard pair of catapults forward.

The advent of the angled deck, which was tested by the US Navy in 1952 on the Essex class carrier *Antietam*, led to the modification of *Forrestal* while building to incorporate this new development. The result was the distinctive configuration which has been adopted by all subsequent US carrier construction: a massive flight deck with considerable overhang supported by sponsons to the sides, with a small island incorporating the smokestack to starboard. The Forrestals were the first US carriers to have the flight deck as the strength deck — in previous ships it was the hangar deck — and in consequence deck-edge

Below: *Ranger* (CV 61) with a full deck-load of aircraft. Although air-defence capabilities have been upgraded with Sea Sparrow and Phalanx, *Ranger* will not now undergo SLEP and may be paid off.

lifts were adopted in preference to centreline lifts and incorporated in the overhang. This resulted in a large uninterrupted hangar in which more than half the ship's aircraft could be struck down. The layout of the four deck-edge lifts proved less than satisfactory, however. In particular the port-side lift, which is at the forward end of the angled deck, cannot be used during landing operations, and the Kitty Hawk class which followed had a modified arrangement.

All four ships of the class were completed with eight 5in (127mm) single gun mountings on sponsons fore and aft. During the 1970s the guns were removed and the sponsons remodelled to receive the Mk 25 BPDMS.

The Forrestals were the first US carriers to undergo the Service Life Extension Program (SLEP), which involved refurbishment of hulls and machinery, and updating of electronics. *Saratoga* (CV 60) was in dockyard hands from 1980 to 1983, *Forrestal* (CV 59) from 1983 to 1985, and *Independence* (CV 62) from 1985 to 1988. All now have two (CV 59/60) or three (CV 51/62) Mk 29 launchers for Sea Sparrow and three Phalanx CIWS. The original radars have been replaced by SPS-48C 3-D and SPS-49, and they have received Mk 23 TAS. Further improvements are planned, including the fitting of Kevlar armour, the replacement of the original Mk C7/C11 catapults by the more powerful C-13, improved tactical data systems, and a Tactical Flag Command Center (TFCC).

Ranger (CV 61), the only ship not to undergo SLEP, may now pay off in 1993. She currently serves with the Pacific Fleet, as does *Independence* (CV 62), which will be home-ported at Yokosuka (Japan) from 1991. The other two ships serve in the Atlantic; *Forrestal* (CV 59) is due to replace the old carrier *Lexington* in the training role in early 1992.

Below: The enormous hangar deck of *Ranger* (CV 61) can accommodate approximately half the vessel's air group.

Above: These F/A-18 Hornet dual-role fighter/attack aircraft belong to the air wing of *Independence* (CV 60), part of over 500 in service.

Submarines

SSBN
Ohio.

Completed:	1981 onwards.
Names:	SSBN 726 *Ohio*; SSBN 727 *Michigan*; SSBN 728 *Florida*; SSBN 729 *Georgia*; SSBN 730 *Henry M. Jackson*; SSBN 731 *Alabama*; SSBN 732 *Alaska*; SSBN 733 *Nevada*; SSBN 734 *Tennessee*; SSBN 735 *Pennsylvania*; SSBN 736 *West Virginia*; SSBN 737 *Kentucky*; SSBN 738 *Maryland*†; SSBN 739 *Nebraska*†; SSBN 740 *Rhode Island*†; SSBN 741 *Maine*†; SSBN 742†; SSBN 743†. (†*building*)
Displacement:	16,765t surfaced; 18,750t submerged.
Dimensions:	Length 560ft oa (170.7m); beam 42ft (12.8m); draught 36ft 6in (11.1m).
Propulsion:	One-shaft nuclear; one S8G reactor with turboeduction drive; 60,000shp = 20 + kts.
Armament:	24 Trident C-4/D-5 SLBMs; four 21in (533mm) torpedo tubes Mk 68 (Mk 48 torpedoes).
Sensors:	*Surveillance:* BPS-15A. *Sonars:* BQQ-6 (see notes), BQS-15, BQR-19.

The original requirement for the Ohio class came from a need to replace the SSBNs of the George Washington and Ethan Allen classes, which were incapable of conversion to fire the current Poseidon or the projected Trident missiles. There was by the early 1970s concern regarding the dramatic growth in Soviet anti-submarine capabilities, which threatened many of the SSBN patrol areas favoured by the US Navy. Forward deployment from European bases, which exposed the US SSBNs to pre-emptive attack in wartime, and to terrorist attack in peacetime, was also increasingly questioned. The Trident C-4 missile which was developed as a successor to Poseidon therefore featured a significant increase in range to 4,000 + nm (7,400km). Available sea-space for SSBN patrol operations was thereby extended from three million to 14 million square miles, and submarines armed with the missile would no longer have to operate from forward bases in order to target the major cities of the Soviet Union. Initially the new SSBN design was to have been an enlarged and improved Lafayette, employing the same S5W reactor for a maximum speed of only 19-20kts. However, the US Navy was anxious to instal a natural circulation reactor based on the model being tested in the *Narwhal* (SSN-671). The desire for sophisticated noise reduction techniques led in turn to a proposal that the expense involved in efficient quieting could be better justified if the missile complement was raised from the original 16 to 24. The result was a submarine more than twice the size of the Lafayette, with a 60,000shp reactor.

The propulsion machinery is extremely quiet in operation. The large S8G natural circulation reactor drives two sets of turbines, one for high and the other for low speed, via a turboeduction drive system. All noise-emitting machinery is raft-mounted and isolated from the hull.

The Trident I C-4 missile is a three-stage solid-fuel rocket carrying eight 100kT MIRVed nuclear warheads. Since 1980 some missiles have had an alternative payload comprising six Mk 500 Evader MARVs (Manoeuvrable Re-entry Vehicles) developed by Lockheed. The Trident I C-4 is currently being superseded by the Trident II D-5, a larger missile with improved throw-weight and accuracy. Range is reported to be 6,000nm (11,100km) with a CEP of only 400ft (122m). The D-5 will carry up to 14 MIRVs of 150kT each, with an alternative payload of seven 300kT MARVs. *Tennessee* (SSBN 734) was the first to be fitted for the Trident

Above: The formidable Ohio class is now the US Navy's standard ballistic missile submarine (SSBN).

Overleaf: The launch tubes for the 24 Trident C-4 missiles, currently being replaced by the more powerful D-5, are abaft the sail.

D-5 missile, which will be retro-fitted to earlier units at two-year intervals.

Sonar capabilities were accorded a higher priority than in earlier SSBNs, and the Ohios have a similar arrangement to that of US Navy SSNs, with a large spherical bow array complemented by amidships torpedo tubes. The BQQ-6 sonar suite is similar to the BQQ-5 suite installed in the Los Angeles class, but without the active component. It comprises a spherical BQS-13 passive ranging sonar for fire-control, a BQR-25 conformal hydrophone array, a PUFFS spot hydrophone array for fire-control, and a BQR-23 towed array.

The Ohio class was designed for 66 per cent availability. The submarines conduct 70-day patrols punctuated by 25-day maintenance periods; there is a 9-year interval between refits, which are programed to last 12 months. The first eight boats are based at a specially-built facility at Bangor, Washington, on the West Coast. Later units are to be based at Kings Bay, Georgia. As a result of the START Treaty only 18 submarines of this class will now be built, and it is envisaged that these will make up the entire US Navy SSBN force by the year 2000.

SSBN

Lafayette

Completed: 1963-67.
Names: SSBN 627 *James Madison*; SSBN 629 *Daniel Boone*; SSBN 630 *John C. Calhoun*; SSBN 632 *Von Steuben*; SSBN 633 *Casimir Pulaski*; SSBN 634 *Stonewall Jackson*; SSBN 640 *Benjamin Franklin*; SSBN 641 *Simon Bolivar*; SSBN 643 *George Bancroft*; SSBN 655 *Henry L. Stimson*; SSBN 657 *Francis Scott Key*; SSBN 658 *Mariano G. Vallejo*.
Displacement: 7,350t surfaced; 8,250t submerged.
Dimensions: Length 425ft (129.5m); beam 33ft (10.1m); draught 29ft (8.8m).
Propulsion: One-shaft nuclear; one S5W reactor driving geared steam turbines; 15,000shp = 20 + kt.
Armament: 16 Trident C-4 SLBMs; four 21in (533mm) torpedo tubes Mk 65 (Mk 48 torpedoes).
Sensors: *Surveillance*: BPS-15.
Sonars: BQR-21, BQS-4, BQR-7, BQR-15 towed array.

The Lafayette was the standard US Navy SSBN throughout the 1960s and 1970s, and had a major influence on the design of other Western SSBNs, notably the British Resolution and the French Le Redoutable classes. Thirty-one were completed between 1963 and 1967.

They were designed to conduct 68-day patrols punctuated by a 32-day maintenance period, with a 16-month refit every six years. Some boats are now on a nine-year refit cycle. Their sensor outfits have been updated, the original BQR-2C passive array being replaced by BQR-21. The last 12 units of the class (officially known as the Benjamin Franklin class), incorporated improvements in machinery noise insulation, some of which have been extended to earlier boats.

Twelve units were modified to enable them to receive the 4,000-plus nm (7,413km) Trident C-4 missile between 1979 and 1982. The refit involved modifications to the launch tubes and the fire-control system, and the installation of keel ballast to compensate for the additional weight. These boats are all home-ported at Kings Bay, Georgia, and will eventually be replaced by later units of the Ohio class. The remaining Poseidon boats left service in late 1991.

Above: *Daniel Webster* (SSBN 626), one of the earliest boats armed with Poseidon; she was retired from service in October 1991.

Below: An HH-46A helicopter overflies *George Washington Carver* (SSBN 656) in the Mediterranean Sea to drop supplies.

Seawolf

Completed:	Building.
Names:	SSN 21 *Seawolf*
Displacement:	7,460t surfaced; 9,150t submerged.
Dimensions:	Length 326ft (96.4m); beam 42ft (12.9m); draught 36ft (10.9m).
Propulsion:	One-shaft nuclear; one S6W reactor driving pump jet; 60,000shp = 35 + kts.
Armament:	Eight 30in (762mm) torpedo tubes (50 Tomahawk, Harpoon missiles, Mk 48 torpedoes).
Sensors:	*Sonars:* BQQ-5D, TB-23 towed array.

Designed to conduct extended patrols in Arctic waters, the Seawolf is the largest and most sophisticated attack submarine to be built for the US Navy. Whereas other attack submarines are relatively noisy at higher speeds, the Seawolf will be capable of travelling at 20kts while virtually silent. This will not only make detection difficult, but will enable the Seawolf to make more effective use of its own passive sensors, which will not be masked by self-noise. The S6W reactor, specifically developed for this class, will power a pump jet propulsor, which will replace the conventional propeller.

The Seawolf has a low length/beam ratio for high manoeuvrability. The bow fins are retractable to facilitate under-ice operations, and there are six stern fins to give fine control. Great emphasis has been placed on reliability and ease of

maintenance, and it is envisaged that these submarines will operate for 15 years before their first refit.

The weapons reload capacity is more than double that of the Los Angeles class, to enable the Seawolf to conduct lengthy operations in hostile waters without replenishment. The eight launch tubes are of greater diameter than previous models in order to accommodate future weapons. A single 30in (762mm) tube has been fitted for trials aboard the Los Angeles class submarine *Memphis* (SSN 691).

The BQQ-5D Wide Aperture Array (WAA) passive sonar suite has been undergoing trials aboard the Los Angeles class submarine *Augusta* (SSN 710) since 1987. The Seawolf will also have the Submarine Active Detection System (SADS), comprising bow-mounted MF and HF active sonars. These sensors will be integrated by an advanced all-digital combat system designated BSY-2, which is currently under development.

The Seawolf has been plagued by development problems related to the high-technology involved, and also to the shift in US Navy requirements resulting from the collapse of the Soviet threat. Originally 29 hulls were to have been built at a rate of 1.5 per year, but the programme has now been reduced to a single boat, to be employed as a technology demonstrator, and it is currently envisaged that the Seawolf will be superseded by a much smaller and less expensive type, the Centurion.

Below: Artist's impression of the advanced Seawolf submarine. Plagued by high costs, of up to a billion dollars, and technology-development problems, construction will now be restricted to a single unit as a technology tester.

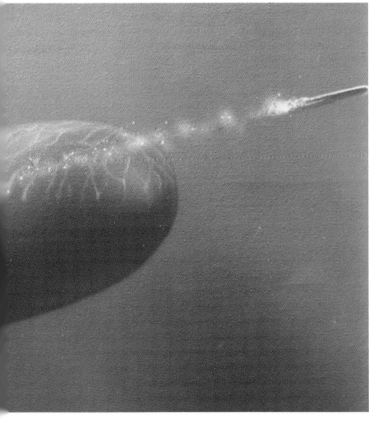

Los Angeles

Completed: 1976 onwards.

Names: SSN 688 *Los Angeles*; SSN 689 *Baton Rouge*; SSN 690 *Philadelphia*; SSN 691 *Memphis*; SSN 692 *Omaha*; SSN 693 *Cincinnati*; SSN 694 *Groton*; SSN 695 *Birmingham*; SSN 696 *New York City*; SSN 697 *Indianapolis*; SSN 698 *Bremerton*; SSN 699 *Jacksonville*; SSN 700 *Dallas* ; SSN 701 *La Jolla*; SSN 702 *Phoenix*; SSN 703 *Boston*; SSN 704 *Baltimore*; SSN 705 *City of Corpus Christi*; SSN 706 *Abuquerque*; SSN 707 *Portsmouth*; SSN 708 *Minneapolis-Saint Paul*; SSN 709 *Hyman G. Rickover*; SSN 710 *Augusta*; SSN 711 *San Francisco*; SSN 712 *Atlanta*; SSN 713 *Houston*; SSN 714 *Norfolk*; SSN 715 *Buffalo*; SSN 716 *Salt Lake City*; SSN 717 *Olympia*; SSN 718 *Honolulu*; SSN 719 *Providence*; SSN 720 *Pittsburgh*; SSN 721 *Chicago*; SSN 722 *Key West*; SSN 723 *Oklahoma City*; SSN 724 *Louisville*; SSN 725 *Helena* SSN 750 *Newport News*; SSN 751 *San Juan*; SSN 752 *Pasadena*; SSN 753 *Albany*; SSN 754 *Topeka*; SSN 755 *Miami*; SSN 756 *Scranton*; SSN 757 *Alexandria*; SSN 758 *Asheville*; SSN 759 *Jefferson City*; SSN 760 *Annapolis*; SSN 761 *Springfield*†; SSN 762 *Columbus*†; SSN 763 *Santa Fe*†; SSN 764 *Boise*†; SSN 765 *Montpelier*†; SSN 766 *Charlotte*†; SSN 767 *Hampton*†; SSN 768 *Hartford*†; SSN 769 *Toledo*†; SSN 770 *Tucson*†; SSN 771 *Columbia*†; SSN 772 *Greeneville*†; SSN 773 *Cheyenne*†.
(†building)

Displacement: 6,080t surfaced; 6,925t submerged.

Dimensions: Length 360ft (109.8m); beam 33ft (10m); draught 32ft 4in (9.8m).

Propulsion: One-shaft nuclear; one S6G reactor driving geared steam turbines; 30,000shp = 30+kts.

Armament: 12 vertical launch tubes Mk 36 for Tomahawk SSMs (SSN 719 onwards); four 21in (533mm) torpedo tubes Mk 67 (22 Tomahawk, Harpoon SSMs, Mk 48 torpedoes).

Sensors: *Surveillance*: BPS-15A.
Sonars: BQQ-5A, BQS-15, BQR-23/25 towed array.

Above: *City of Corpus Christi* (SSN 705) running on the surface in the Atlantic Ocean. The class has a diving depth of 1,475ft (450m).

Left: *Oklahoma City* (SSN 723), built at Newport News SB & DD Co in 1984/85. Later units of the class will have bow-mounted diving planes.

In the late 1960s the US Navy became increasingly concerned about the threat to its carrier battle groups posed by the new generation of Soviet submarines, and in particular the Charlie class SSGN with its SS-N-7 "pop-up" missile. Thus was born the "close-support" mission which provided the rationale for the development of the Los Angeles class. The ability to operate in conjunction with the carrier battle groups required high tactical speed, which in the Thresher/Permit and Sturgeon classes had been sacrificed in favour of quiet operation. However, the new submarine would also need to be at least as quiet as its immediate predecessors in order to engage in underwater combat with the Soviet SSGNs. The result was an exceptionally large boat with double the reactor power of earlier types.

The S6G reactor is a modified version of the D2G reactor used to power missile destroyers since the early 1960s. It employs natural circulation at low power ratings to minimise pump noise, but circulation pumps have to be switched on at higher speeds. This fits well into the pattern of "sprint and drift" operations implied in the close-support mission. The large size of the submarine has facilitated the effective isolation of noise-generating machinery from the hull, and the Los Angeles is probably the world's quietest nuclear submarine.

The fin is relatively small in relation to the overall size of the submarine, thereby reducing resistance. However, the ability to rotate the fin-mounted hydroplanes to the vertical has been sacrificed, and this has placed limitations on under-ice

Below: An officer mans the periscope on a submarine of the Los Angeles class during a red alert. There are 13 officers in the highly trained compliment of 133 men.

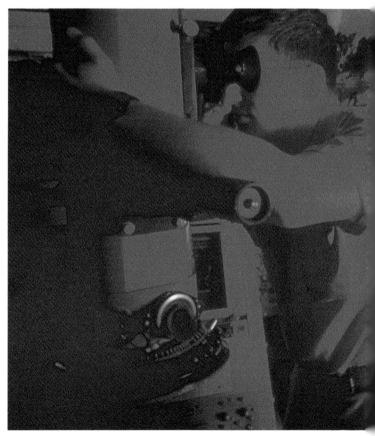

operations. From SSN 751 onwards the hydroplanes are being moved to the bow. These later boats are typed the 688I (for "Improved") class, and are designed to be fully "Arctic-capable". They have acoustic tile cladding. SSN 768 onwards will have many of the advanced features of the Seawolf class, including improved quieting, additional stern fins, and improved propulsion systems.

The first 12 units received the Mk 113 fire-control system; later units have the all-digital Mk 117, which permits Harpoon launch. The submarine-launched variant of the Harpoon anti-ship missile entered service aboard this class in 1978. The first operational installation of the Tomahawk missile dates from 1983. All submarines of the class carry eight Tomahawk missiles together with Harpoon SSMs and Mk 48 torpedoes; SSN 719 and later have 12 Mk 36 vertical launch tubes for Tomahawk located in the space between the bow sonar and the forward end of the pressure hull.

The Los Angeles class was designed from the outset to accommodate the BQQ-5 sonar suite. Like the BQQ-2 system which it replaces, the BQQ-5 is based on a large active/passive spherical bow sonar, a conformal passive hydrophone array, and a PUFFS fire-control system. The BQS-11/12/13 spherical bow array incorporates Digital Multi-Beam Steering (DIMUS), which has superseded the mechanical scanning employed with earlier sonars and makes possible multi-target tracking. Another new feature of the BQQ-5 sonar suite is the addition of a BQR-23/25 towed array, which is stowed in a tube along the hull casing.

Fifty-three submarines of this class had been completed by the end of 1991, with a further nine building or on order, making this the largest class of nuclear submarine ever built. A further four units due to be authorized under FY 90-92 were cancelled due to the defence cuts.

Sturgeon

Completed:	1967-75.
Names:	SSN 637 *Sturgeon*; SSN 638 *Whale*; SSN 639 *Tautog*; SSN 646 *Grayling*; SSN 647 *Pogy*; SSN 648 *Aspro*; SSN 649 *Sunfish*; SSN 650 *Pargo*; SSN 652 *Puffer*; SSN 653 *Ray*; SSN 660 *Sandlance*; SSN 661 *Lapon*; SSN 662 *Gurnard*; SSN 663 *Hammerhead*; SSN 665 *Guitarro*; SSN 666 *Hawkbill*; SSN 667 *Bergall*; SSN 668 *Spadefish*; SSN 669 *Seahorse*; SSN 670 *Finback*; SSN 672 *Pintado*; SSN 673 *Flying Fish*; SSN 674 *Trepang*; SSN 675 *Bluefish*; SSN 676 *Billfish*; SSN 677 *Drum*; SSN 678 *Archerfish*; SSN 679 *Silversides*; SSN 680 *William H. Bates*; SSN 681 *Batfish*; SSN 682 *Tunny*; SSN 683 *Parche*; SSN 684 *Cavalla*; SSN 686 *Mendel Rivers*; SSN 687 *Richard B. Russell*.
Displacement:	4,250/4,460t surfaced (see remarks); 4,780/4,960t submerged.
Dimensions:	Length 292ft/302ft (89m/92.1m); beam 31ft 8in (9.7m); draught 29ft (8.8m).
Propulsion:	One-shaft nuclear; one S5W reactor driving geared steam turbines; 15,000shp = 26kts.
Armament:	Four 21in (533mm) torpedo tubes Mk 63 (23 Tomahawk, Harpoon SSMs, Mk 48 torpedoes).
Sensors:	*Surveillance*: BPS-14/15. *Sonars*: BQQ-2/BQQ-5, BQS-14A, BQR-23/25 towed array.

The Sturgeon, developed via the Thresher/Permit class, was the standard US Navy SSN design of the 1970s. As compared with its predecessors, the Sturgeon was enlarged to provide the necessary internal volume for more effective quieting and additional electronics.

The general arrangement of the Thresher/Permit class was adopted, with the bow occupied by the BQS-6 spherical array and the torpedo tubes angled

Below: *Pintado* **(SSN 672), one of a number of submarines of the class modified to carry a deep submergence rescue vehicle.**

out beneath the fin. The fin-mounted hydroplanes are 38ft (11.6m) wide and can be rotated to the vertical to enable the submarines to break through ice.

Early units of the class received the BQQ-2 sonar suite, comprising the BQS-6 active/passive spherical bow array, the BQR-7 conformal passive array, and a PUFFS fire control sonar. The last nine units were lengthened by 10ft (3m) to facilitate the installation of the advanced BQQ-5 sonar suite and its associated electronics. As earlier units are retro-fitted with the new system they too are being lengthened.

The original Mk 113 fire-control system is being replaced by the all-digital Mk 117, which permits Harpoon launch. Some units have been fitted to carry Deep Submergence Rescue Vehicles (DSRV), and SSN 679 and SSN 687 have the Bustle prototype communications buoy in a container abaft the fin. Anechoic hull coatings have been applied to several boats.

Two units of this class (SSN 651 *Queenfish* and SSN 664 *Sea Devil*) paid off prematurely in 1991 to save the cost of refuelling and refitting them.

Above: *Ray* (SSN 653), *Hawkbill* (SSN 666) and *Archerfish* (SSN 678) after the first simultaneous submarine surfacing at the North Pole.

Cruisers

CG
Ticonderoga

Completed:	1983 onwards.
Names:	CG 47 *Ticonderoga*; CG 48 *Yorktown*; CG 49 *Vincennes*, CG 50 *Valley Forge*; CG 51 *Thomas S. Gates*; CG 52 *Bunker Hill*; CG 53 *Mobile Bay*; CG 54 *Antietam*; CG 55 *Leyte Gulf*; CG 56 *San Jacinto*; CG 57 *Lake Champlain*; CG 58 *Philippine Sea*; CG 59 *Princeton*; CG 60 *Normandy*; CG 61 *Monterey*; CG 62 *Chancellorsville*; CG 63 *Cowpens*; CG 64 *Gettysburg*; CG 65 *Chosin*; CG 66 *Shiloh*; CG 67 *Hue City*; CG 68 *Anzio*†; CG 69 *Vicksburg*†; CG 70 *Lake Erie*†; CG 71 *Cape St George*†; CG 72 *Vella Gulf*†; CG 73 *Port Royal*†. († *building*)
Displacement:	8,910t standard; 9,465t full load.
Dimensions:	Length 567ft oa (172.8m); beam 55ft (16.8m); draught 22ft (6.5m).
Propulsion:	Two-shaft COGAG; four LM 2500 gas turbines; 80,000bhp = 30kts.
Armament:	*AAW*: Two twin Mk 26 launchers (44 + 44) for Standard SM-2 MR missiles in CG 47-51; two Mk 41 Mod 0 vertical launch systems (61 + 61) for Standard SM-2 MR missiles in CG 52-73; two Mk 15 Phalanx CIWS. *ASW*: ASROC missiles from Mk 26 launcher in CG 47-51; two LAMPS I/III helicopters; six 12.75in (324mm) torpedo tubes Mk 32 (2 × 3). *ASuW*: Eight Harpoon missiles (2 × 4); Tomahawk missiles from Mk 41 VLS in CG 52-73; two 5in (127mm) Mk 45 D-P guns (2 × 1).
Sensors:	*Surveillance*: Four SPY-1A/B, SPS-49, SPS-55. *Fire-Control*: Four SPG-62, SPQ-9A. *Sonars*: SQS-53A/B/C, SQR-19 towed array.

Below: *Ticonderoga* **(CG 47), the name-ship of the class, transits the Suez Canal during September 1990 en route to the Gulf.**

Above: *Bunker Hill* (CG 52), the first of the class to be fitted with the Mk 41 vertical launch system (VLS) in programme Baseline I.

Below: *Normandy* (CG 60) entered service in December 1989. The Mk 41 VLS houses the SM-2 and Tomahawk missiles.

Ticonderoga (CG 47) was the first operational US Navy ship to be fitted with the Aegis air-defence system. It was originally envisaged that Aegis would be installed in nuclear-powered escorts such as the Strike Cruiser (CSGN) and the CGN 42 variant of the Virginia class, but the enormous cost of combining Aegis with nuclear propulsion proved to be prohibitive under the restrictive budgets of the 1970s. It was eventually decided to utilise the growth potential of the Spruance hull to provide the requisite number of Aegis escorts. The figure of 27 ships completed or building represents three Aegis cruisers per two-carrier battle group (CVBG), and a single Aegis cruiser for each of four surface action groups (SAG), based around one of the four recommissioned battleships of the Iowa class (two of which are now being returned to the Naval Reserve Force while *Missouri* and *Wisconsin* remain for the moment).

Aegis was developed to counter the saturation missile attacks which could be expected to form the basis of Soviet anti-carrier tactics during the 1980s. Conventional rotating radars are limited both in data rate and in number of target tracks they can handle, whereas saturation missile attacks require sensors which can react immediately and have a virtually unlimited tracking capacity. The solution adopted in the Aegis system is to mount four fixed planar antennae each covering a sector of 45 degrees on the superstructures of the ship. Each SPY-1 array has more than 4,000 radiating elements that shape and direct multiple beams. Targets satisfying predetermined criteria are evaluated, arranged in sequence

of threat and engaged, either automatically or with manual override, by a variety of defensive systems.

At longer ranges air targets are engaged by the Standard SM-2 MR missile, which differs from earlier missiles in requiring target illumination only in the terminal phase of flight. In the initial and mid-flight phase the missile flies under auto-pilot towards a predicted interception point. The four Mk 80 illuminators are slaved to the system and can, through time-sharing, serve more than 12 missiles in the air simultaneously. Because the SM-2 missile has a more economical flight profile than previous missiles engagements are possible at ranges approaching 40nm (74km).

At closer ranges, anti-ship missiles "leaking" through missile defences are countered by a combination of electronic countermeasures and the Mk 15 Phalanx CIWS. The 5in (127mm) guns can engage surface or shore targets up to a distance of 12.6nm (23km) but have no anti-air capability, as their Mk 86 gun fire-control system (GFCS) lacks the SPG-60 radar required for the effective engagement of aerial targets.

Ticonderoga and her sisters are designed to serve as flagships, and have an elaborate Combat Information Center (CIC) equipped with large vertical displays,

Below: *Mobile Bay* (CG 53) during sea trials in the Gulf of Mexico. Each of the two Mk 41 VLS has a maximum capacity of 61 missiles.

Above: An SM-2 air-defence missile is launched from the after Mk 26 launcher of *Ticonderoga* (CG 47).

which can accept and coordinate data both from the ship's own sensors and from other ships and aircraft, and transmit data directly to other task force assets in order to co-ordinate surface actions.

In order to incorporate the latest equipment as it becomes available the class has been divided into five sub-groups. *Vincennes* (CG 49) was the first ship to be fitted with the RAST haul-down and traverse system to enable her to operate the LAMPS III SH-60B Seahawk. She also had the improved Block 2 missile.

The first five ships have two conventional Mk 26 twin-arm launchers, but from *Bunker Hill* (CG 52) these have been replaced by Mk 41 Mod 0 vertical launch systems (VLS), each of which can accommodate 61 missiles. The early ships can fire the ASROC missile, 20 rounds being stowed in the forward Mk 26 magazine. The Mk 41 VLS fitted to the later ships can accommodate Tomahawk.

San Jacinto (CG 56) will be the first ship to have the SQQ-89(V)3 integrated ASW suite, incorporating the SQS-53B hull sonar, the SQR-19 towed array and Mk 116 Mod 6 fire-control. Later ships will have the lighter SPY-1B array, which has improved radiating characteristics, and UKK-43B and UYK-44 computers will replace the original UYK-7/20 computer suite.

The more extensive superstructures and equipment required to support the Aegis system, together with the provision of Kevlar armour over the vital spaces, have brought these ships close to their maximum full load displacement. The first two ships were fitted with a small quantity of keel ballast to preserve their stability, but this has been dispensed with in later units of the class.

Below: The air/surface picture is monitored on the PT-525 large screen displays aboard the well-equipped *Vincennes* (CG 49).

Virginia

Completed:	1976-80.
Names:	CGN 38 *Virginia*; CGN 39 *Texas*; CGN 40 *Mississippi*; CGN 41 *Arkansas*.
Displacement:	10,400t light; 11,300t full load.
Dimensions:	Length 582ft oa (177.3m); beam 63ft (19.2m); draught 24ft (7.4m).
Propulsion:	Two-shaft nuclear; two D2G reactors driving geared steam turbines; 60,000shp = 30kts.
Armament:	*AAW*: Two twin Mk 26 launchers (44 + 24) for Standard SM-2 MR missiles; two Mk 15 Phalanx CIWS.
	ASW: ASROC missiles from fwd Mk 26 launcher; six 12.75in (324mm) torpedo tubes Mk 32 (2 × 3).
	ASuW: Eight Tomahawk missiles (2 × 4); eight Harpoon missiles (2 × 4); two 5in (127mm) Mk 45 D-P guns (2 × 1).
Sensors:	*Surveillance*: SPS-48A/C/E, SPS-40/49, SPS-55.
	Fire-Control: Two SPG-51D, SPG-60D, SPQ-9A.
	Sonar: SQS-53A.

Following closely upon the two CGNs of the California class, the *Virginia* incorporated a number of significant modifications. While the basic layout of the class is identical to that of their predecessors, the single-arm Mk 13 launchers of the *California* were superseded by the new Mk 26 twin ASROC launcher forward, and a helicopter hangar was built into the stern.

The magazine layout and missile-handling arrangements of the Mk 26 constitute a break with previous US Navy practice. In earlier missile cruisers and destroyers booster-assisted missiles such as Terrier were stowed in horizontal magazine rings, and the shorter Tartar missiles in cylindrical magazines comprising two concentric rings of vertically stowed missiles. The magazine associated with the Mk 26 launcher, however, has a continuous belt feed system with vertical stowage capable of accommodating a variety of missiles. This means that ship's length is the only limiting factor on the size of the magazine, which is capable of being "stretched" or "contracted" to suit the dimensions of the vessel in which it is to be installed. It has also eliminated the requirement for a separate launcher for ASROC. In the Virginia class ASROC rounds are carried in the forward magazine alongside Standard MR surface-to-air missiles. The elimination of the ASROC

Below: *Mississippi* **(CGN 40), during the Gulf War. Note the armoured quadruple box launchers for the Tomahawk land attack misssile (TLAM) on the quarterdeck, fitted at the expense of helicopters.**

Above: *Arkansas* (CGN 41), prior to the installation of its armoured box launchers for Tomahawk in the late 1980s.

Below: *Texas* (CGN 39). The twin-arm Mk 26 launcher is restricted to the unboosted variant of the SM-2 missile but will be improved.

launcher and its associated reloading deckhouse has saved 5m (16.4ft) in length compared with *California*.

The Virginia class also differs from the *California* in having the solid-state SQS-53 hull sonar in place of SQS-26, and the all-digital Mk 116 ASW fire-control system instead of the analogue Mk 114. Only two SPG-51D illuminators were fitted, as it was envisaged from the outset that these ships would convert to the SM-2 missile, which requires target illumination only in the terminal phase of flight. All ships of the class are due to receive the New Threat Upgrade (NTU), in which the SPS-48A/C radars will be upgraded to SPS-48E and the SYS-2 Integrated Automatic Detection and Tracking (IADT) System will be installed, by 1995.

Harpoon missiles were fitted forward of the bridge structure during the early 1980s, when two Mk 15 Phalanx CIWS were added abeam the plated foremast. Subsequently the helicopter facilities were removed and two armoured box launchers for Tomahawk located atop the original hangar. Kevlar armour was added over vital topside and magazine spaces during refits in FY82-86.

The original requirement was for 11 ships of this class, which would then combine with earlier CGNs to provide each of the CVANs projected at that time with four nuclear-powered escorts. After only four units of the class had been laid down, however, further orders were suspended while consideration was given first to the Strike Cruiser (CSGN) and then to a modified CGN 38 design with Aegis (CGN 42). Both projects were eventually abandoned in favour of the conventionally-powered *Ticonderoga* (CG 47).

Virginia (CGN 38) and *Mississippi* (CGN 40) currently serve in the Atlantic, and the other two ships in the Pacific.

Below: *Virginia* (CGN 38). There was to have been an Aegis variant of the design (CGN 42), but the project was abandoned.

California

Completed:	1974-75.
Names:	CGN 36 *California*; CGN 37 *South Carolina*.
Displacement:	9,675t light; 10,530t full load.
Dimensions:	Length 596ft oa (182m); beam 61ft (18.6m); draught 24ft (7.4m).
Propulsion:	Two-shaft nuclear; two D2G reactors driving geared steam turbines; 60,000shp = 30kts.
Armament:	*AAW*: Two single Mk 13 launchers (40 + 40) for Standard SM-2 MR missiles; two Mk 15 Phalanx CIWS. *ASW*: ASROC launcher Mk 112 (1 × 8, reloads); four 12.75in (324mm) torpedo tubes Mk 32 (4 × 1, fixed). *ASuW*: Eight Harpoon missiles (2 × 4); two 5in (127mm) Mk 45 D-P guns (2 × 1).
Sensors:	*Surveillance*: SPS-48C, SPS-40B, SPS-67. *Fire-Control*: Four SPG-51D, SPG-60, SPQ-9A. *Sonars*: SQS-26CX.

Below: *California* **(CGN 36) and her sister are due to receive the full NTU upgrade during the early 1990s, funds permitting.**

California and her sister *South Carolina* were built in response to the need for a new class of nuclear escorts to accompany the CVNs of the Nimitz class. A third ship was approved in FY 1968, but this was later cancelled in favour of the improved Virginia design.

Compared with previous CGNs, *California* is a much larger, more sophisticated vessel. The design reverted to the "double-ended" layout of *Bainbridge*, but single Mk 13 Tartar launchers were adopted in preference to the Mk 10. This was in some ways a retrograde step in that it limited the ships to the medium-range (MR) version of the Standard missile, whereas earlier CGs and CGNs could be retro-fitted with the extended-range (ER) version. It also necessitated the provision of a separate ASROC launcher, forward of which there is a magazine surmounted by a prominent deckhouse into which the missiles are hoisted prior to reloading.

California was the first ship to receive the lightweight 5in Mk 45 gun. The all-digital Mk 86 FC system employs separate SPQ-9A and SPG-60 radars for anti-surface and anti-air engagements respectively. The SPG-60 can also be employed as a fifth illuminating channel for the Standard missiles. Harpoon missiles, Mk 15 Phalanx CIWS and Kevlar armour were fitted during the 1980s, and both ships are to receive a major NTU upgrade (see Virginia class).

Both ships began their service lives in the Atlantic, but *California* (CGN 36) was transferred to the Pacific in the early 1980s. In service they have served as battle group escorts for both nuclear and fossil-fuelled carriers.

Belknap

Completed:	1964-67.
Names:	CG 26 *Belknap*; CG 27 *Josephus Daniels*; CG 28 *Wainwright*; CG 29 *Jouett*; CG 30 *Horne*; CG 31 *Sterett*; CG 32 *William H. Standley*; CG 33 *Fox*; CG 34 *Biddle*.
Displacement:	6,570t standard 8,065t full load.
Dimensions:	Length 547ft oa (166.7m); beam 55ft (16.7m); draught 19ft (5.9m).
Propulsion:	Two-shaft geared steam turbines; 85,000shp = 33kts.
Armament:	*AAW*: twin Mk 10 launcher (60) for Standard SM-2 ER missiles; two Mk 15 Phalanx CIWS. *ASW*: One SH-2F LAMPS I helicopter (not in CG 26); ASROC missiles from Mk 10 launcher; six 12.75in (324mm) torpedo tubes Mk 32 (2 × 3). *ASuW*: Eight Harpoon missiles (2 × 4); one 5in (127mm) Mk 42 D-P gun.
Sensors:	*Surveillance*: SPS-48E, SPS-49, SPS-67. *Fire-Control*: Two SPG-55D, SPG-53A. *Sonar*: SQS-26BX (CG 26; SQS-53A).

The nine ships of the Belknap class, together with their nuclear powered half-sister *Truxtun* constitute the final group of AAW "frigates" completed for the US Navy during the 1960s. Outwardly they resemble their predecessors of the Leahy class, with which they share a common hull-form and superstructure layout. A closer look, however, reveals a shift in emphasis in favour of significantly increased anti-submarine capabilities.

In the Belknaps the "double-ended" missile launcher arrangement was abandoned and the 5in (127mm) gun reinstated — a reflection, in part, of concern about the diminishing number of vessels capable of fire support operations.

Right: *Horne* (CG 30), still with her original SPS-43 air surveillance radar (now replaced by SPS-49 during New Threat Upgrade).

Below: *Jouett* (CG 29) operating in the Gulf, with GDC Pomona Standard SM-2 ER missiles loaded onto the Mk 10 launcher forward.

The Mk 10 Terrier launcher was given a third 20-round magazine ring located below and between the other two. The extra capacity was used, however, not to compensate for the reduction in Terrier rounds compared with the Leahy, but in order to dispense with a separate ASROC launcher. The upper two rings carry alternate Terrier/Standard and ASROC rounds, while the third, which carries only SAM rounds, serves as a feed for the two upper rings.

The additional deck space gained as a result of these modifications was utilised to provide a helicopter platform and hangar immediately abaft of the second mack. It was envisaged that the Belknaps would operate the ill-fated drone anti-submarine helicopter (DASH) but the programme was abandoned before any drones were embarked. Instead, the Belknaps became the trial class for the LAMPS helicopter programme in the early 1970s, and introduced manned ASW helicopters to the US Navy with conspicuous success.

The Belknaps carried a more advanced electronics outfit than earlier US Navy carrier escorts, and were the first US Navy ships to have the computer-based Naval Tactical Data System. *Wainwright* (CG 28) was the trials ship for the SM-2 ER variant of the Standard missile, which is now carried by all ships of the class.

Belknap (CG 26), which had her entire upper works destroyed by fire following a collision with the *John F. Kennedy* (CV 67) in 1975, was completely rebuilt with an upgraded sensor outfit. In a subsequent refit 1985-86 she was equipped to serve as 6th Fleet Flagship, with enhanced communications and staff accommodations at the expense of the helicopter hangar. Three other units (CG 28, CG 30 and CG 31) were fitted with a Tactical Flag Command Center (TFCC) during the same period.

Below: A recent view of *Horne* (CG 30), now with two quad Harpoon launchers, two Mk 15 Phalanx and the Raytheon SPS-49 radar.

All ships had their original 3in (76mm) AA mountings replaced by Harpoon SSMs from 1976 onwards. They will retain their SH-2F LAMPS I helicopters, but are currently receiving the full NTU upgrade (see Virginia Class), which will enable them to engage aerial targets with their Standard ER missiles out to ranges of 90-100nm.

CG 26-28 and CG 34 currently serve in the Atlantic, and the other five ships in the Pacific. They are routinely assigned as Anti-Air Warfare (AAW) escorts to the carrier battle groups.

Above: *Fox* (CG 33). These ships have been extensively modernised and are receiving the NTU upgrade, due to complete by late 1993.

CGN
Bainbridge

Completed: 1962.
Names: CGN 25 *Bainbridge*.
Displacement: 8,000t light; 9,100t full load.
Dimensions: Length 565ft oa (172.2m); 58ft (17.7m); draught 25ft (7.7m).
Propulsion: Two-shaft nuclear; two D2G reactor driving geared steam turbines; 60,000shp = 30kts.
Armament: *AAW*: Two twin Mk 10 launchers (40 + 40) for Standard SM-2 ER missiles; two Mk 15 Phalanx CIWS.
ASW: ASROC launcher Mk 112 (1 × 8); six 12.75in (324mm) torpedo tubes Mk 32 (2 × 3).
ASuW: Eight Harpoon missiles (2 × 4).
Sensors: *Surveillance*: SPS-48C, SPS-49, SPS-67.
Fire-Control: Four SPG-55C.
Sonar: SQQ-23.

Bainbridge is a near-sister of the Leahy class, with which she initially shared an identical outfit of weapons and electronics. As completed, she presented a more streamlined profile than the Leahy because nuclear propulsion enabled her to dispense with the tall macks of the latter.

The layout of *Bainbridge's* weapons is identical to that of the *Leahy*, with twin Mk 10 Terrier launchers fore and aft and an ASROC box launcher forward of the bridge. From 1974 onwards the ship underwent an extensive refit aimed at upgrading her electronics. Harpoon missiles replaced the original 3in (76mm) AA guns, and the Naval Tactical Data System (NTDS) was installed in a new after superstructure block. Further upgrading during the 1980s has included the fitting of two Mk 15 Phalanx CIWS, the replacement of the original SPS-37 air surveillance radar by SPS-49, and the updating of her electronic warfare suite. She can now fire the SM-2 variant of the Standard missile.

Bainbridge currently serves in the Atlantic Fleet, but is due to decommission in FY 94. The *Truxtun* (CGN 35), a nuclear-powered variant of the Belknap class, is due to decommission in FY 92. Although she received a major modernisation from 1982 to 1984, the cost of further overhauling her nuclear propulsion machinery was probably the main factor in her early demise.

Above: *Bainbridge* (CGN 25) was the US Navy's first nuclear-powered AAW escort. She has recently undergone modernisation.

Below: *Bainbridge* underway in the Pacific. Note the "double-ended" missile launcher layout and the absence of major guns.

CG
Leahy

Completed:	1962-64.
Names:	CG 16 *Leahy*; CG 17 *Harry E. Yarnell*; CG 18 *Worden*; CG 19 *Dale*; CG 20 *Richmond K. Turner*; CG 21 *Gridley*; CG 22 *England*; CG 23 *Halsey*; CG 24 *Reeves*.
Displacement:	6,070t standard 8,200t full load.
Dimensions:	Length 553ft oa (162.4m); beam 53ft (16.2m); draught 19ft (5.9m).
Propulsion:	Two-shaft geared steam turbines; 85,000shp = 32kts.
Armament:	*AAW:* Two twin Mk 10 launchers (40 + 40) for Standard SM-2 ER missiles; two Mk 15 Phalanx CIWS.
	ASW: ASROC launcher Mk 112 (1 × 8); six 12.75in (324mm) torpedo tubes Mk 32 (2 × 3).
	ASuW: Eight Harpoon missiles (2 × 4).
Sensors:	*Surveillance:* SPS-48E, SPS-49, SPS-10/67.
	Fire-Control: Four SPG-55C.
	Sonar: SQS-23 (SQQ-23B in CG 17).

The nine ships of the Leahy class, together with their nuclear-powered half-sister *Bainbridge*, constitute the second group of AAW "frigates" completed for the US Navy during the 1960s.

They were designed at a time when it was thought that guns would disappear altogether from the inventory of naval weapons. They were therefore the first US Navy ships to have an all-missile main armament. They also introduced the "mack" (combined mast and stack) to US Navy construction as a means of conserving valuable centreline deck space.

Right: A stern view of *Leahy* (CG 16) in the Pacific. This class has already undergone two major AAW modernisations.

Below: *Halsey* (CG 23). The "double-ended" missile layout distinguishes these ships from the later Belknap class.

A "double-ended" layout was adopted with twin Mk 10 Terrier launchers fore and aft. There are 20-round magazine rings in line with each launcher arm, and the missiles are lifted from the top of the ring and run up at an angle of 15 degrees through a wedge-shaped deckhouse onto the launcher.

There is a separate eight-round ASROC launcher forward of the bridge, but no reloads are carried, neither do these ships carry a helicopter. *Harry E. Yarnell* (CG 17) has received the SQQ-23B PAIR (Performance And Integration Refit) sonar, which incorporates both active and passive transducers in a single hull dome, but the other units retain the original SQS-23.

From 1967 until 1972 the Leahy class underwent an extensive modernisation programme aimed at bringing their electronics up to the same standard as the Belknaps. A large planar SPS-48 3-D radar replaced the original SPS-39, and NTDS was installed. *Dale* (CG 19) received an SPS-49 radar in place of the original SPS-43 in 1976; the other units were similarly modified in the early 1980s. At the same time the original 3in (76mm) guns were replaced by Harpoon, two Mk 15 Phalanx CIWS were installed on platforms projecting from the sides of the after superstructure, and the ECM outfit was upgraded to include SLQ-32(V)3.

By 1985 all ships of the class had been modified to enable them to fire the Standard SM-2 ER missile. They subsequently received the full NTU upgrade (see Virginia class), with the SPS-48E radar and the SYS-2 weapon control system.

CG 17, CG 19, CG 20, and CG 22 currently serve in the Atlantic, and the remaining five ships in the Pacific. Although completed almost 30 years ago, these ships remain first-line units because of the upgrading of their air-defence systems.

Below: *Halsey* as she appeared in the late 1970s, prior to the installation of the Phalanx Close In Weapons Systems (CIWS) and Harpoon Surface-to-Surface Missiles (SSM) to replace the original 3in guns. The New Threat Upgrade modernisation was completed in 1991 and included updating of the Mk 10 launchers.

Above: *Leahy* (CG 16) underway in the Pacific. The large square planar antenna atop the forward "mack" is for the SPS-48 3-D radar. In this pre-modernisation view *Leahy* has the SPS-43 two-dimensional air surveillance radar, since replaced by SPS-49, atop the after "mack". The fire-control radars have now also been improved with SPG-55.

Long Beach

Completed:	1961.
Name:	CGN 9 *Long Beach*.
Displacement:	15,540t light; 17,525t full load.
Dimensions:	Length 721ft oa (219.8m); beam 73ft (22.3m); draught 31ft max (9.5m).
Propulsion:	Two-shaft nuclear; two CIW reactors driving geared steam turbines; 80,000shp = 30kts.
Armament:	*AAW*: Two twin Mk 10 launchers (40 + 80) for Standard SM-2 ER missiles; two Mk 15 Phalanx CIWS.
	ASW: ASROC launcher Mk 112 (1 × 8); six 12.75in (324mm) torpedo tubes Mk 32 (2 × 3).
	ASuW: Eight Tomahawk missiles (2 × 4); eight Harpoon missiles (2 × 4); two 5in (127mm) Mk 30 guns.
Sensors:	*Surveillance*: SPS-48C, SPS-49, SPS-67.
	Fire-Control: Four SPG-55D.
	Sonar. SQQ-23.

Long Beach was the US Navy's first all-missile warship, and the first surface ship with nuclear power. She was designed as an escort for the carrier (CVN 65) *Enterprise*, and has performed this role well.

As completed she had two Mk 10 Terrier launchers forward and a Mk 12 launcher aft for the long-range Talos missile. The depth of the hull enabled an extra pair of magazine rings to be worked in beneath the second Mk 10 launcher, giving *Long Beach* a total capacity of no fewer than 166 surface-to-air missiles. There was an ASROC box launcher amidships, and shortly after the ship entered service two 5in (127mm) guns of an older pattern were fitted to provide defence against small surface craft. Electronics were on a par with *Enterprise* herself, with large fixed SPS-32/33 ''billboard'' radars mounted on a similar ''turret'' superstructure block.

A proposal in the mid-1970s to refit *Long Beach* with the Aegis system was abandoned on grounds of cost. Talos was removed in 1979 and replaced by Harpoon. The following year the ship began a major refit at which the original ''billboard'' arrays were removed and replaced by conventional rotating radar antennae, aluminium armour was added to the forward superstructure, and two Mk 15 Phalanx CIWS were fitted in place of the former SPG-49 Talos FC radars. Armoured box launchers for Tomahawk were fitted above the stern in 1985, and the fire-control system was modified to enable the Standard SM-2 ER missile to be fired.

At her next refit *Long Beach* is due to receive a full NTU upgrade, a Tactical Flag Command Center (TFCC), and additional armour. She serves in the Pacific.

Above: *Long Beach* (CGN 9) has been extensively modernised and up-armed, with Tomahawk, Harpoon and Phalanx being fitted aft.

Below: *Long Beach* in the Gulf. The original SPS-32/33 "billboard" planar arrays were replaced in 1980, along with the ship's computer.

Destroyers

DDG
Arleigh Burke

Completed:	1991 onwards.
Names:	DDG 51 *Arleigh Burke*; DDG 52 *Barry*†; DDG 53 *John Paul Jones*†; DDG 54 *Curtis Wilbur*†; DDG 55 *Stout*†; DDG 56 *John S. McCain* †; DDG 57 *Mitscher* †; DDG 58 *Laboon*‡; DDG 59 *Russell*‡; DDG 60 *Paul Hamilton*‡; DDG 61 *Ramage* ‡; DDG 62 *Fitzgerald*‡; DDG 63 *Stethem*‡; DDG 64-67 ‡. († building ‡ projected)
Displacement:	6,680t light; 8,375t full load.
Dimensions:	Length 504ft 6in oa (153.8m); beam 67ft (20.4m); draught 20ft (6.1m).
Propulsion:	Two-shaft COGAG; four LM2500 gas turbines; 100,000hp = 30 + kts.
Armament:	*AAW*: Two Mk 41 Mod 0 vertical launch systems (29 + 61) for Standard SM-2 MR missiles; two Mk 15 Phalanx CIWS. *ASW*: Six 12.75in (324mm) torpedo tubes Mk 32 (2 × 3). *ASuW*: Eight Harpoon missiles (2 × 4); Tomahawk missiles from Mk 41 VLS: one 5in (127mm) Mk 45 D-P gun.
Sensors:	*Surveillance*: Four SPY-1D, SPS-67. *Fire-Control:* Three SPG-62. *Sonars*: SQS-53C, SQR-19 towed array.

Above: *Arleigh Burke* **(DDG 51) is the first of a new series of battle-group capable anti-air warfare destroyers. The US Navy wants 32.**

Above: The launch of *Arleigh Burke* at Bath Ironworks in September 1989. A further 12 are on order, six of them at Ingalls Shipbuilding.

Intended as a replacement initially for the Charles F. Adams and Coontz classes, the Arleigh Burke was designed as a battle-group-capable general purpose destroyer. An exceptionally lengthy development phase has been followed by delays in construction due to labour problems at the Bath Iron Works shipyard. The first unit (authorised in 1985) was completed only in 1991, by which time many of the ships due for replacement had already been retired from service.

The Arleigh Burke has approximately 75 per cent of the air-defence capability of the Ticonderoga class cruiser. There are Mk 41 vertical launch systems for the SM-2 MR and Tomahawk missiles fore and aft, but the forward Mk 41 VLS comprises only four eight-cell modules instead of eight, thereby reducing magazine capacity from 122 to 90 missiles. The SPY-1D planar arrays are a more advanced, lightweight design, but there are only three Mk 80 illuminators.

Anti-submarine warfare capabilities are significantly reduced as compared with the Ticonderoga. The SQQ-89(V)4 integrated sonar suite, comprising the SQS-53C hull sonar, the SQR-19 towed array and the SQQ-28 helicopter data link, is the most advanced in the US Navy. However, the only ASW weapons system currently operational is the Mk 46 homing torpedo. Vertical launch ASROC was to have been fired from the Mk 41 VLS, but the programme has been cancelled. The ships have no helicopter hangar. This was a conscious decision taken in order to minimise displacement and cost, the theory being that there would be sufficient helicopter assets on other task group escorts, and that the new destroyers would therefore require only "cross-decking" facilities. DDG 52 onwards will be fitted with a RAST haul-down system, and will have helicopter

refuelling and rearming facilities. Later ships of the class (unit 24 on) may have a helicopter hangar for two SH-60B at the expense of the SQR-19 towed array.

The design of these ships was heavily influenced by a 1979 Defense Science Board study of warship vulnerability. Whereas US Navy warships of the previous generation relied on the sophistication of their weapons systems to protect them against damage, the Arleigh Burke design places considerable emphasis on "passive" protection. Construction, including superstructures, is almost exclusively of steel, with 130 tons of Kevlar armour over vital spaces. These are the first US Navy ships to have a gas-tight "citadel", all spaces having positive pressurisation to keep out NBC contaminants. The Combat Information Center (CIC) is located within the hull, contrary to previous US Navy practice, and is surrounded by passageways. The distributed data-processing architecture ensures that the ship's weaponry cannot be disabled by a single hit, and the sonar room is placed well forward away from the CIC.

An exceptionally broad hull-form has been adopted in order to maximise deck-space and improve sea-keeping. This has not been without cost; these ships require 25 per cent more power than the Ticonderogas to drive them at their maximum speed of 30 knots, and endurance is only 4,200nm (7,778km) at 20 knots, considerably less than that of other contemporary battle group escorts.

Below: Arleigh Burke running speed trials. The SPY-1D Aegis planar arrays are located at the four corners of the single superstructure block. The angled surfaces and round edges are Stealth technology.

Kidd

Completed:	1981-82.
Names:	DDG 993 *Kidd*; DDG 994 *Callaghan*; DDG 995 *Scott*; DDG 996 *Chandler*.
Displacement:	6,950t light; 9,575t full load.
Dimensions:	Length 563ft oa (171m); beam 55ft (16.8m); draught 23ft (7m).
Propulsion:	Two-shaft COGAG; four LM2500 gas turbines; 80,000hp = 30kts.
Armament:	*AAW*: Two twin Mk 26 launchers (24 + 44) for Standard SM-2 MR missiles; two Mk 15 Phalanx CIWS.
	ASW: One SH-2F LAMPS I helicopter; ASROC missiles from after Mk 26 launcher; six 12.75in (324mm) torpedo tubes Mk 32 (2 × 3).
	ASuW: Eight Harpoon missiles (2 × 4); two 5in (127mm) Mk 45 D-P guns.
Sensors:	*Surveillance*: SPS-48E, SPS-49, SPS-55.
	Fire-Control: Two SPG-51D, SPG-60, SPQ-9A.
	Sonar: SQS-53A.

The four ships of the Kidd class are AAW modifications of the Spruance class destroyer originally ordered by Iran but acquired by the US Navy in 1979 following the fall of the Shah.

The allowances made in the Spruance design for the modular installation of a number of weapon systems then in production or under development made redesign a simple matter, as the AAW modification had been one of the variations originally envisaged. In the Kidd class twin-arm Mk 26 launchers have been fitted fore and aft in place of the ASROC and Sea Sparrow launchers of the ASW version. The forward magazine is the smaller of the two, the original intention being to fit the now defunct 8in (205mm) Mk 71 gun in place of the forward 5in (127mm) mounting. Sixteen ASROC missiles are carried in the 44-round after magazine, giving an ASW capability close to that of the Spruance.

Shortly after completion the Kidd class received Harpoon SSMs and two Mk 15 Phalanx CIWS. The original electronics outfit was austere by US Navy standards. This was subsequently remedied when the class underwent full NTU upgrades 1987-1990. In addition to the advanced SPS-48E radar and the SYS-2 weapons data system, the Kidds have received an SPS-49 long-range air surveillance radar. This has replaced the SPG-60 FC radar on the foremast platform, the latter being relocated to a new platform projecting from the mainmast. These modifications, together with the addition of Kevlar and aluminium armour, have raised displacement by 1,000 tons.

Kidd (DDG 993) and *Scott* (DDG 995) serve in the Atlantic, and the other two ships in the Pacific.

Below: The four AAW destroyers of the Kidd class were originally ordered by Iran, but were purchased at a very competitive price following the ousting of the Shah by revolutionary forces. This is *Chandler* (DDG 996), last of the group of four.

Spruance

Completed:	1975-80.
Names:	DD 963 *Spruance*; DD 964 *Paul F. Foster*; DD 965 *Kinkaid*; DD 966 *Hewitt*; DD 967 *Elliott*; DD 968 *Arthur W. Radford*; DD 969 *Peterson*; DD 970 *Caron*; DD 971 *David W. Ray*; DD 972 *Oldendorf*; DD 973 *John Young*; DD 974 *Comte De Grasse**; DD 975 *O'Brien*; DD 976 *Merrill**; DD 977 *Briscoe*; DD 978 *Stump*; DD 979 *Conolly**; DD 980 *Moosbrugger*; DD 981 *John Hancock*; DD 982 *Nicholson*; DD 983 *John Rodgers**; DD 984 *Leftwich**; DD 985 *Cushing**; DD 986 *Harry W. Hill*; DD 987 *O'Bannon*; DD 988 *Thorn*; DD 989 *Deyo**; DD 990 *Ingersoll**; DD 991 *Fife*; DD 992 *Fletcher*; DD 997 *Hayler*.
Displacement:	5,915t light; 8,040t full load.
Dimensions:	Length 563ft oa (171m); beam 55ft (16.8m); draught 19ft (5.9m).
Propulsion:	Two-shaft COGAG, four LM2500 gas turbines; 80,000hp = 30 + kts.
Armament:	*ASW*: One SH-2F LAMPS I or SH-6OB LAMPS III helicopter; ASROC launcher Mk 112 (1 × 8, 24 missiles); six 12.75in (324mm) torpedo tubes Mk 32 (2 × 3). *ASuW*: Mk 41 Mod 0 vertical launch system (61) for Tomahawk missiles (not in *); eight Tomahawk missiles (2 × 4)*; eight Harpoon missiles (2 × 4); two 5in (127mm) Mk 45 D-P guns. *AAW*: Sea Sparrow launcher Mk 29 (1 × 8, 16 reloads); two Mk 15 Phalanx CIWS.
Sensors:	*Surveillance*: SPS-40B/C/D (SPS-49 in DD 997), SPS-55. *Fire-Control*: SPG-60, SPQ-9A, Mk 91. *Sonars*: SQS-53B/C, SQR-19 towed array.

Below: *Deyo* (DD 989) prior to the installation of the Mk 15 Phalanx CIWS which has six 20mm barrels.

Above: An early view of the sixth of class, *Arthur W. Radford* (DD 968). The FMC 5in gun is capable of 20 rounds per minute.

Below: *Kinkaid* (DD 965) with Phalanx CIWS installed *en echelon* atop the bridge and the helicopter hangar for one SH-60B or SH-2F.

The most controversial ships to be built for the US Navy since World War II, the Spruance class was designed to replace the war-built destroyers of the Gearing and Allen M. Sumner classes, which had undergone FRAM ASW modification programmes during the 1960s but by the early 1970s were nearing the end of their useful lives.

At 8,040t full load — twice the displacement of the destroyers it was to replace — the *Spruance* epitomised the US Navy's design philosophy of the 1970s. This philosophy envisaged the construction of large hulls with block superstructures which maximised internal volume, fitted out with machinery that could be easily maintained and, if necessary, replaced, and equipped with high-technology weapon systems that could be added to and updated by modular replacement at a later stage. The object was to minimise "platform" costs, which have no military pay-off, in favour of greater expenditure on weapon systems ("payload") in order to ensure that the ships would remain first-line units throughout the 30-year life-expectancy of their hulls.

In a further attempt to minimise "platform" costs the entire class was ordered from a single shipbuilder, the Litton/Ingalls Corporation, which invested heavily in a major production facility at Pascagoula, using advanced modular construction techniques.

The only "visible" weapons aboard *Spruance* when she was completed were 5in (127mm) Mk 45 lightweight gun mountings fore and aft and an ASROC box launcher forward of the bridge. In view of the size and cost of the ships this caused an immediate public outcry.

The advanced ASW qualities of the Spruance class are, however, largely hidden within the hull and the bulky superstructures. The ASROC launcher (fitted to all ships on completion) has a magazine directly beneath it in which 16 reloads are stowed vertically. The large hangar to port of the after funnel uptakes (since widened to accommodate the SH-60B Seahawk) can accommodate two LAMPS helicopters side by side. The triple Mk 32 tubes concealed behind hull doors are served by handling-rooms and a magazine for 18 Mk 46 torpedoes. Moreover the solid-state SQS-53 bow sonar, which can operate in a variety of active and passive modes, including direct path, bottom bounce and convergence zone, has proved so successful that the original plan to fit SQS-35 VDS in these ships was abandoned.

The all-gas-turbine propulsion system, which employs paired LM2500 turbines *en echelon* in a unit arrangement, is complemented by gas-turbine generators. This has resulted in a significant reduction in underwater noise emission, together with reduced maintenance and manning requirements.

The other feature of these ships which was not immediately apparent was the enormous growth potential built into the design in order to accommodate a variety of weapons systems then at the development stage. Shortly after completion they received the Sea Sparrow Improved Point Defense Missile System (IPDMS), Harpoon anti-ship missiles, Mk 15 Phalanx CIWS, and the

Below: *John Young* (DD 973). In most units of this class the ASROC launcher is being replaced by a Mk 41 vertical launch system (VLS).

Above: *Ingersoll* (DD 990) is one of eight ships recently armed with quadruple armoured box launchers for Tomahawk.

advanced SLQ-32 EW system. Subsequently, during the mid-1980s, eight ships (see table) were fitted with armoured box launchers for Tomahawk, and all were fitted with Kevlar armour.

From FY 86 onwards the remaining ships of the class began to have their ASROC launcher and its associated magazine removed, to be replaced by a Mk 41 Mod 0 vertical launch system. Tomahawk surface-to-surface missiles will be accommodated in the VLS, with a future option of Standard SM-2 missiles controlled by an accompanying Aegis ship. All ships of the class are being fitted with the Mk 23 TAS to enable them to detect low-flying aircraft and missiles, the principal threats to modern ships.

As a result of these modifications full load displacement has risen by more than 1,000 tons, and the number of enlisted men has risen from 232 to 315. The flexibility of the Spruance design is such that it has formed the basis both for the AAW destroyers originally ordered for Iran (see Kidd class) and for the Ticonderoga class.

Hayler (DD 997), the last ship of the class, was originally to have had increased hangar and flight deck space for helicopter and VTOL operations, but this modification found greater favour with Congress than with the US Navy, which subsequently decided to complete the ship to the standard Spruance configuration. *Hayler* has since run trials of the Litton automated engine-control system intended for the Arleigh Burke class.

Below: Data from the Mk 23 TAS Target Designation Radar is displayed at a UYA-4 weapons control console.

Frigates

FFG
Oliver Hazard Perry

Completed: 1977 onwards.
Names: FFG 7 *Oliver H. Perry*; FFG 8 *McInerney*;
FFG 9 *Wadsworth*; FFG 10 *Duncan*; FFG 11 *Clark*;
FFG 12 *George Philip*; FFG 13 *Samuel E. Morison*;
FFG 14 *Sides*; FFG 15 *Estocin*; FFG 16 *Clifton Sprague*;
FFG 19 *John A. Moore*; FFG 20 *Antrim*; FFG 21 *Flatley*;
FFG 22 *Fahrion*; FFG 23 *Lewis B. Puller*;
FFG 24 *Jack Williams*; FFG 25 *Copeland*; FFG 26 *Gallery*;
FFG 27 *Mahlon S. Tisdale*; FFG 28 *Boone*;
FFG 29 *Stephen W. Groves*; FFG 30 *Reid*; FFG 31 *Stark*;
FFG 32 *John L. Hall*; FFG 33 *Jarrett*; FFG 34 *Aubrey Fitch*;
FFG 36 *Underwood*; FFG 37 *Crommelin*; FFG 38 *Curts*;
FFG 39 *Doyle*; FFG 40 *Halyburton*; FFG 41 *McCluskey*;
FFG 42 *Klakring*; FFG 43 *Thach*; FFG 45 *De Wert*;
FFG 46 *Rentz*; FFG 47 *Nicholas*; FFG 48 *Vandegrift*;
FFG 49 *Robert G. Bradley*; FFG 50 *Taylor*; FFG 51 *Gary*;
FFG 52 *Carr*; FFG 53 *Hawes*; FFG 54 *Ford*; FFG 55 *Elrod*;
FFG 56 *Simpson*; FFG 57 *Reuben James*;
FFG 58 *Samuel B. Roberts*; FFG 59 *Kauffman*; FFG 60
Rodney M. Davis; FFG 61 *Ingraham*.
Displacement: 2,770t/3,010t light; 3,660t/4,100t full load.
Dimensions: Length 445/455ft oa (135.6/138.8m); beam 45ft (13.7m);
draught 19ft (5.8m).
Armament: *AAW*: single Mk 13 launcher (40) for Standard SM-1 MR
missiles; one 76mm Mk 75 D-P gun; one Mk 15 Phalanx
CIWS.
ASW: One/two SH-60B LAMPS III helicopters; six 12.75in
(324mm) torpedo tubes Mk 32 (2 × 3).
ASuW: Harpoon missiles from Mk 13 launcher.
Sensors: *Surveillance*: SPS-49, SPS-55.
Fire-Control: STIR (modified SPG-60).
Sonar: SQS-56, SQR-18/19 towed array (not in all).

**Above: The frigates *Oliver Hazard Perry* (FFG 7), *Antrim* (FFG 20) and
Jack Williams (FFG 24) in a staggered formation.**

Above: The single-arm Mk 13 launcher fires the SM-1 missile, with the fire-control being provided by a modified SPG-60 (Lockheed STIR).

The FFG 7 design has its origins in the Patrol Frigate first proposed in September 1970. The latter was to constitute the "low" end of the so-called "high/low" mix, providing large numbers of cheap second-rate escorts with reduced capabilities to counterbalance the sophisticated but costly specialist ASW and AAW vessels whose primary mission was to protect the carriers. Strict limitations were therefore imposed on cost, displacement and manpower requirements.

Unlike its near-contemporary, the high-value Spruance class, which had its own specialised production facility, the FFG 7 was designed to be built anywhere. Simple construction techniques were encouraged, making maximum use of flat panels and bulkheads, and passageways are generally straight. The hull structure can be prefabricated in modules of 35, 100, 200 or 400 tons, allowing the various shipyards to use the most convenient size. As a result the programme ran to schedule, some units even being delivered early, and costs were close to the original estimates. Adoption of the USAF-derived "fly-before-buy" concept resulted in a two-year gap between completion of the first ship and the rest of the class, enabling initial problems to be ironed out and modifications incorporated in follow-on units.

Like the frigates which preceded her, the Oliver Hazard Perry has a "second-class" propulsion plant on one screw. The layout is, however, much more compact than that of the Knox as a result of the adoption of gas turbines. Two LM2500s — the same model as that installed in the Spruance — are located side-by-side in a single engine room. Two small retractable propulsion pods fitted just abaft the sonar dome provide back-up during docking procedures, and these can drive the ship at 6 knots in an emergency.

The balance of the armament is more closely oriented to AAW than that of the Knox, which was a specialist ASW design. The FFG 7 has a Mk 13 launcher forward for Standard MR surface-to-air missiles and Harpoon anti-ship missiles, and an OTO-Melara 76mm (3in) quick-firing gun atop the bulky superstructure block. ASROC has been abandoned altogether, but there is a broad hangar aft for two LAMPS helicopters. Although intended from the outset to operate the SH-60B Seahawk LAMPS III, which is equipped to provide over-the-horizon guidance for the Harpoon SSMs in addition to its ASW duties, early units were equipped to handle only the older-model SH-2F LAMPS I, FFG-36 onwards (together with FFG-8, which served as trials ship) have an extended flight deck,

Above: The units which operate the SH-60B LAMPS III have extended flight decks aft which do not add to the waterline length.

Left: Stern view of *Curts* (FFG 38), showing the double helicopter hangar, with Kevlar armour, surmounted by a Phalanx CIWS.

Below: *Crommelin* (FFG 37) and her later sisters have fin stabilizers to provide a steady helicopter platform in a rolling sea.

Above: *Taylor* (FFG 50) operating in the Gulf, where two ships of this class sustained severe damage in separate incidents.

and SH-60B support equipment, fin stabilizers and a RAST haul-down system. The latter permits launch and recovery with a roll of 28deg and a pitch of 5deg.

The original SQS-56 sonar was conceived as an austere model with neither the long range nor the multi-mode capability of the larger SQS-26/53 series, FFG-36 onwards were to have received an upgraded SQQ-89 sonar suite incorporating an SQR-19 towed array and the SQQ-28 helicopter sonobuoy data link system, but delays with the SQQ-89 processor have resulted in an interim outfit based on the SQR-18 towed array in several ships.

During the 1980s all received the Mk 15 Phalanx CIWS, and Kevlar and aluminium armour was fitted over the magazine, command and machinery spaces. The original complement of 17 officers and 167 enlisted men was found to be too small to run the ship, and later ships have 30 additional berths.

During the late 1980s many of the earalier units were transferred to the Naval Reserve Force (NRF); those still in active service are being brought up to the same standard as later units of the class. As a result of modifications these ships are some 450 tons overweight. They have nevertheless proved exceptionally robust when subjected to action damage, as evidenced by the survival of the *Stark* (FFG 31, struck by two Iraqi Exocet missiles in May 1987) and the *Samuel B. Roberts* (FFG-58, mined in the Gulf in April 1988).

Below: ***John L. Hall* (FFG 32) transits the Suez Canal during 1990. She has the extended flight deck for helicopter usage.**

Knox

Completed:	1969-74.
Names:	FF 1052 *Knox*; FF 1053 *Roark*; FF 1054 *Gray*;
	FF 1055 *Hepburn*; FF 1056 *Connole*; FF 1057 *Rathburne*;
	FF 1058 *Meyerkord*; FF 1059 *W.S. Sims*; FF 1060 *Lang*;
	FF 1061 *Patterson*; FF 1062 *Whipple*; FF 1063 *Reasoner*;
	FF 1064 *Lockwood*; FF 1065 *Stein*;
	FF 1066 *Marvin Shields*; FF 1067 *Francis Hammond*;
	FF 1068 *Vreeland*; FF 1069 *Bagley*; FF 1070 *Downes*;
	FF 1071 *Badger*; FF 1072 *Blakely*;
	FF 1073 *Robert E. Peary*; FF 1074 *Harold E. Holt*;
	FF 1075 *Trippe*; FF 1076 *Fanning*; FF 1077 *Ouellet*;
	FF 1078 *Joseph Hewes*; FF 1079 *Bowen*; FF 1080 *Paul*;
	FF 1081 *Aylwin*; FF 1082 *Elmer Montgomery*;
	FF 1083 *Cook*; FF 1084 *McCandless*;
	FF 1085 *Donald B. Beary*; FF 1086 *Brewton*;
	FF 1087 *Kirk*; FF 1088 *Barbey*; FF 1089 *Jesse L. Brown*;
	FF 1090 *Ainsworth*; FF 1091 *Miller*;
	FF 1092 *Thomas C. Hart*; FF 1093 *Capodanno*;
	FF 1094 *Pharris*; FF 1095 *Truett*;
	FF 1096 *Valdez*; FF 1097 *Moinester*.
Displacement:	3,075t light; 4,260t full load.
Dimensions:	Length 440ft oa (134m); beam 47ft (14.3m); draught 16ft (4.6m).
Armament:	*ASW*: One SH-2F LAMPS I helicopter; ASROC launcher Mk 112 (1 × 8, reloadable); four 12.75in (324mm) torpedo tubes Mk 32 (4 × 1).
	AAW: One Mk 15 Phalanx CIWS.
	ASuW: Harpoon missiles from ASROC launcher; one 5in (127mm) Mk 42 D-P gun.
Sensors:	*Surveillance*: SPS-40B, SPS-10/67.
	Fire-Control: SPG-53.
	Sonars: SQS-26CX, SQS-35 VDS (some ships), SQR-18A towed array.

Above: *Roark* (FF 1053), displaying her reloadable eight-cell Mk 112 launcher for ASROC. She is now in the Naval Reserve Force.

Below: *Pharris* (FF 1094). The telescopic hangar for the SH-2F Seasprite anti-submarine helicopter extends onto the flight deck.

The Knox class began as a Design Work Study of the Brooke class missile escort. Congressional opposition to the mounting costs of fitting escorts with the Tartar system resulted, however, in the abandonment of the latter class after only six units had been laid down, The *Knox* was therefore redesigned as an ASW Escort.

Although the *Knox* retained the one-shaft propulsion system of the Garcia/Brooke design, the complex pressure-fired boilers of the latter were abandoned in favour of a "safer", more conventional steam plant. This necessitated an increase in size without creating any extra space for weapons.

Originally the two 5in (127mm) Mk 38 guns of the *Garcia* were to have been replaced by a combination of a single 5in Mk 42 and the ill-fated Sea Mauler point-defence missile. The Sea Mauler was eventually replaced by the Sea Sparrow BPDMS — a system not contemplated when the *Knox* was designed.

Other "hiccups" in the development of the *Knox* include the abandonment of a fixed "billboard" ECM antenna which influenced the design of the tall mack, of the pair of fixed torpedo tubes (for Mk 37/Mk 48 torpedoes) which were to have been fitted in the stern, and of the DASH drone anti-submarine helicopter programme.

Below: *Brewton* (FF 1086) at Pearl Harbor, Hawaii, during a ceremony to honour those servicemen who lost their lives in Vietnam.

Ultimately the abandonment of DASH worked to the ships' advantage as it was replaced by the LAMPS I manned helicopter. As with the previous two classes of escort, the hangar received a telescopic extension. Taken together with the reloadable ASROC launcher and the SQS-26 sonar, this gave the *Knox* a first-class anti-submarine outfit, which rescued the design from an unpromising beginning.

The ASROC magazine can now stow the Harpoon SSM, which is launched from the port pair of missile cells in the Mk 112 launcher. During the 1980s all ships of the class received a single Mk 15 Phalanx CIWS in place of the Mk 25 BPDMS (never fitted in FF 1084-97), and the SQS-35 variable depth sonar was modified to permit towing of the SQR-18 passive array. Ships not fitted with the SQS-35 received a modified version of the SQR-18. Electronic warfare equipment was updated and the SPS-10 radar was upgraded to SPS-67. Bow bulwarks and a hull strake were fitted to reduce wetness forward. A proposal to upgrade the SQS-26CX sonar and the Mk 114 FC system was abandoned because of cost.

With the reduced requirement for operational ocean escorts, the Knox class is steadily being transferred into the Naval Reserve Force (NRF); 18 ships had been transferred by mid-1991, and it is envisaged that the remaining ships will be decommissioned by 1994.

Patrol Combatants

Pegasus

Completed:	1977-83.
Names:	PHM 1 *Pegasus*; PHM 2 *Hercules*; PHM 3 *Taurus*; PHM 4 *Aquila*; PHM 5 *Aries*; PHM 6 *Gemini*.
Displacement:	198t light; 235-241t full load.
Dimensions:	Length 133ft oa (40.5m); beam 28ft (8.6m); draught 6ft (1.9m).
Propulsion:	One LM2500 gas turbine (foilborne); 16-19,000shp = 50kts; two MTV diesels (hullborne); 1,340bhp = 12kts.
Armament:	Eight Harpoon (2 × 4); one 3in (76mm) MK 75.
Sensors:	*Surveillance*: SPS-64. *Fire-Control*: Mk 92 (Mk 94 in PHM 1).

The PHM was one of the four new designs in the "low" programme advocated in Zumalt's Project 60 (see Introduction). It was envisaged that squadrons of these fast patrol craft would be deployed at the various choke-points — in particular those in the Mediterranean and the north-west Pacific — through which the surface units of the Soviet Navy needed to pass in order to reach open waters. High speed and a heavy armament of anti-ship missiles would enable the PHM to make rapid interceptions, and the relatively low unit cost meant that large numbers could be bought.

Technical problems with the hydrofoil system resulted in cost increases, and opponents of the PHM programme, pointing to the limited capabilities of the design, tried to obtain cancellation of all except the lead vessel. Congress insisted, however, on the construction of the six units for which funds had already been authorised.

The propulsion system of the PHM comprises separate diesels driving two waterjets for hullborne operation and a single gas turbine for high-speed foilborne operation.

The Mk 94 GFCS on *Pegasus* was bought direct from HSA but the Mk 92 systems on the other five were manufactured under licence. The original anti-ship missile armamant has been doubled, with two quadruple mounts replacing the four singles first envisaged.

Below: *Hercules* (PHM 2) and *Taurus* (PHM 3) operating at speed in the Gulf of Mexico. Now operating anti-drug patrols their single LM 2500 gas turbine can drive them in pursuits at 50 knots.

Mine Warfare

MHC
Osprey

Completed: Building.
Names: MHC 51 *Osprey*; MHC 52 *Heron*†; MHC 53 *Pelican*†;
MHC 54 *Robin*†; MHC 55 *Oriole*†; MHC 56-59‡.
(† building. ‡ projected.)
Displacement: 895t full load.
Dimensions: Length 188ft (57.3m); beam 35ft (10.6m); draught 9ft
(2.7m).
Propulsion: Two-shaft diesel/electric motors plus bow thruster;
3,200bhp = 12kts.
Armament: One 30/40mm, one 12.7mm gun.
Sensors: *Surveillance*: SPS-64.
Sonar: SQQ-32.

The MHC 51 programme replaces the abortive Cardinal (MSH) project abandoned in 1986. The air-cushion MSH, of which 17 units were projected, failed shock-testing trials. The US Navy considered various existing conventional displacement minehunters under construction in Europe before deciding on a derivative of the Italian Lerici class.

Construction is of heavy GRP throughout with all frames eliminated, and the main machinery is mounted on vibration dampers. Displacement has grown by 110 tons during the final design phase, largely due to the quantity of equipment the US Navy wished to incorporate, and construction is now well behind schedule.

The SQQ-32 minehunting sonar is a joint development between Raytheon and the Thomson Sintra. The British Plessey Nautis-M data handling system will be fitted. The SLQ-48 mine neutralisation system (MNS) is also a feature of the Avenger class (q.v.) Mechanical sweep gear will be carried, and the Modular Influence Sweep System, a towed influence sweep with its own gas-turbine sweep current generator, will be installed when it becomes available.

Seven of the projected 12 units of the class had been authorised by FY 91. It is envisaged that they will be followed by eight modified vessels of greater length. Following a one-year work-up period with naval crews each ship will be passed down to the Naval Reserve Force (NRF).

Below: *Osprey* is the first of a coastal minehunter class based on a modified Italian design and built in Savannah, Georgia, USA.

MCM
Avenger

Completed: 1987 onwards.
Names: MCM 1 *Avenger*; MCM 2 *Defender*; MCM 3 *Sentry*; MCM 4 *Champion*; MCM 8 *Guardian*; MCM 6 *Devastator*; MCM 7 *Patriot*; MCM 8 *Scout*; MCM 9 *Pioneer*†; MCM 10 *Warrior*†; MCM 11 *Gladiator*†; MCM 12 *Ardent*†; MCM 13 *Dexterous*†; MCM 14 *Chief*†. (†Building.)
Displacement: 1,195ft light; 1,312t full load.
Dimensions: Length 224ft (68.3m); beam 39ft (11.9m); draught 12ft (3.7m).
Propulsion: Two-shaft diesel/electric motor plus bow thruster (see notes); 2,400bhp = 13.5kts.
Armament: Two 12.7mm (2 × 1).
Sensors: *Surveillance*: SPS-55.
Sonar: SQQ-30/32.

Below: The first US MCM type to be built for 30 years, the Avenger class has both hunting and sweep gear incorporated.

Designed to replace the 1950s-built Ocean Minesweepers of the Aggressive class, the Avenger was the first US Navy MCM vessel to be built for almost 30 years, and numerous problems have been experienced both with the design and with the equipment to be installed, resulting in lengthy delays and cost overruns.

The hull is of layered and glued wooden planking with a protective Glass Reinforced Plastic (GRP) coating and GRP superstructures. Built both for minehunting and for deep-sea sweeping, the Avenger has a variety of mine counter-measures equipment. Deep-moored mines can be swept to a depth of 180m (98 fathoms) using mechanical sweep gear, and there is an SLQ-37(V)2 magnetic/acoustic sweep array. For minehunting there are two SLQ-48 mine neutralisation systems (MNS). These are remote-controlled submersibles powered by hydraulic motors, which can deposit an explosive charge next to a bottom-laid mine out to 1,500m from the ship.

Problems experienced during construction include: instability (resolved by lengthening the hull by 6ft (1.8m) during construction); poorly manufactured reduction gears; diesel engines which rotated in the opposite direction to the gear-boxes; and difficulties in meeting the stringent electro-magnetic interference requirements.

The first eight units were to have been operated by the Naval Reserve Force (NRF), and the remainder to serve with the active fleet. This decision may be reviewed following US Navy experience of mine warfare during the Gulf Conflict.

Amphibious Warfare Vessels

LCC
Blue Ridge

Completed:	1970-71.
Names:	LCC 19 *Blue Ridge*; LCC 20 *Mount Whitney*.
Displacement:	16,790t light; 18,650t full load.
Dimensions:	Length 636ft oa (194m); beam 82ft wl (25m), 108ft upper deck (32.9m); draught 25ft (7.5m).
Propulsion:	One-shaft steam turbine; 22,000shp = 20kts.
Armament:	Two BPDMS launchers Mk 25 (2 × 8); four 3in (76mm) Mk 33 guns (2 × 2); two Mk 15 Phalanx CIWS.
Sensors:	*Surveillance*: SPS-48C, SPS-40, SPS-67.
	Fire-Control: Two Mk 115.

These two vessels were built to provide specialised command facilities for the amphibious fleets in the Pacific and Atlantic respectively. They replaced the more numerous war-built AGFs, which had inadequate speed for the new 20-knot amphibious squadrons. The basic design is that of the Iwo Jima class LPH, with the former hangar occupied by command spaces, offices and accommodation. Prominent sponsons for LCPLs and ships' boats project from the sides, and the broad flat upper deck is lined with a variety of surveillance, ECM/ESM and communications aerials. The LCCs are fitted with the Naval Tactical Data System (NTDS), the Amphibious Command Information System (ACIS) and the Naval Intelligence Processing System (NIPS). As completed, they had only two twin 3in (76mm) mountings for defence against aircraft, but two BPDMS launchers were added in 1974, and two Mk 15 Phalanx CIWS were fitted 1985-87. Two

utility helicopters are generally operated from the flight pad aft but there are no hangar or maintenance facilities.

The command facilities originally provided for a naval Commander Amphibious Task Group (CATG), a Marine Landing Force Commander (LFC), Air Control Group Commander, and their respective staffs, with accommodation for up to 200 officers and 500 enlisted men in addition to the 780-man crew.

There were plans for a third ship (AGC 21), which would have provided both fleet command and amphibious command facilities, but inadequate speed for fleet work was an important factor in her cancellation. With the demise of the Cleveland class fleet flagships in the late 1970s, however, *Blue Ridge* and *Mount Whitney* became flagships of the Seventh (W. Pacific) and the Second (Atlantic) Fleets respectively. They were subsequently fitted with a Tactical Flag Command Center (TFCC).

Above: *Blue Ridge* **and her sister are fitted with extensive and sophisticated tactical data and communications facilities.**

Below: *Blue Ridge* **(LCC 19) serves as flagship of the US Seventh Fleet, and is home-ported in the Pacific at Yokosuka, Japan.**

LHD
Wasp

Completed:	1989 onwards.
Names:	LHD 1 *Wasp*; LHD 2 *Essex* †; LHD 3 *Kearsage* †; LHD 4 *Boxer* †; LHD 5 . . . †. (†Building.)
Displacement:	28,235t light; 40,530t full load.
Dimensions:	Length 844ft oa (257.3m); beam 106ft wl (32.3m), 140ft flight deck (42.67m); draught 26ft (8.1m).
Propulsion:	Two-shaft geared steam turbines; 70,000shp = 24kts.
Armament:	Two Sea Sparrow launchers Mk 29; three Mk 15 Phalanx CIWS.
Aircraft:	*Assault Mode*: 30 helicopters (CH-53D/E Sea Stallion, CH-46E Sea Knight, AH-1W Sea Cobra, UH-1N Iroquois); six AV-8B Harrier. *Carrier Mode*: 20 AV-8B Harrier; four/six SH-60B LAMPS III.
Troops:	1,873.
Sensors:	*Surveillance*: SPS-52C/48E, SPS-49, SPS-67. *Fire-Control*: Two Mk 91.

Intended as replacements for the Iwo Jima class, the LHDs of the Wasp class are derived from the Tarawa class LHA (q.v.). Like the latter, the Wasps are being built by Ingalls SB at their highly-automated Pascagoula building facility. The first unit was authorised in FY 84 and the fifth under FY 91. The projected programme was for seven hulls, but cuts in defence funding have resulted in cancellation of the last two.

In spite of the external similarities between the Wasp and Tarawa there are important differences in conception, equipment and construction between the two classes. The LHD was designed from the outset to operate the Marine AV-8B Harrier and the LCAC air-cushion landing craft. It was envisaged that the ship would have a multi-purpose role, being equally capable of embarking heavy-lift helicopters for a conventional "vertical assault", a deck-load of AV-8B Harriers for ground support of an amphibious landing, or a combination of AV-8Bs and LAMPS anti-submarine helicopters for "sea control" duties (a mission not dissimilar to that of the abortive SCS design).

The flight deck is constructed of HY 100 steel for additional strength, and the original hangar has been enlarged. A ski-jump ramp was considered but rejected because its adoption would have reduced the number of deck spots

Below: *Wasp* (LHD 1) is the first of a new class of assault ships designed to operate the Marine AV-8B Sea Harrier.

for helicopters. Additional deck-space has been created by deleting the 5in (127mm) guns of the Tarawa, enabling the flight deck to be carried forward at maximum width to the bow. The centreline aircraft lift of the earlier ships has been replaced by a second deck-edge lift, which is located to starboard. Both lifts have a capacity of 34 tons, enabling them to handle the heaviest Marine aircraft.

Other differences include a longer, narrower island superstructure, internal stowage for the ship's boats, and a bulbous forefoot which may be retro-fitted to the Tarawa. The narrow, single-bay docking-well can accommodate three LCAC air-cushion landing craft, each of which has a capacity of 60 tons of vehicles or stores, with an alternative load-out of 12 LCM (6) landing craft. The Wasp has a conventional LSD/LPD-type lowering stern gate whereas the Tarawa has a rising gate. There are six (versus five) cargo elevators, each with dimensions of 25ft × 12ft (7.6m × 3.6m).

A consequence of the increase in the size of the hangar is that vehicle capacity has been reduced by 35 per cent, and there has been a small reduction in dry

cargo space. Hospital facilities, on the other hand have been expanded from 300 to 600 beds, and the Wasp carries more JP-5 aviation fuel to support its larger complement of aircraft.

Embarkation of the LCAC enables amphibious assaults to be conducted over the horizon. Gunfire support would generally be carried out by destroyers operating closer to the shore. This has enabled the Wasp class to dispense with the 5in (127mm) guns of the Tarawa, Sea Sparrow launchers are located at the forward end of the island, and on the centreline beneath the flight deck aft; the Mk 15 Phalanx CIWs are located at the after corners of the flight deck and on the island superstructure. The extensive sensor outfit, which from the second ship will include the advanced SPS-48E 3-D radar, is coordinated by an SYS-2 data/weapons control system.

Below: The Wasp class can be employed as a sea-control ship in addition to its dedicated amphibious assault mission.

LHA
Tarawa

Completed:	1976-80.
Names:	LHA 1 *Tarawa*; LHA 2 *Saipan*; LHA 3 *Belleau Wood*; LHA 4 *Nassau*; LHA 5 *Peleliu*.
Displacement:	25,120t light; 39,300t full load.
Dimensions:	Length 834ft oa (254m); beam 107ft wl (32m) 132ft (40m); draught 26ft (7.9m).
Propulsion:	Two shaft geared steam turbines, 70,000shp = 24kts.
Armament:	Two 5in (127mm) Mk 45 D-P guns (2 × 1); two Mk 15 Phalanx CIWS; six 20mm AA (6 × 1).
Aircraft:	Six CH-53D/E Sea Stallion; 12-16 CH-46D/E Sea Knight; four AH-IT/W Sea Cobra; four UH-IN Iroquois.
Troops:	1,924.
Landing-craft:	Four LCU, two LCM.
Sensors:	*Surveillance*: SPS-52B, SPS-40B, SPS-10F. *Fire-Control*: SPG-60, SPQ-9A, two Mk 115.

The last in a series of ocean-going amphibious vessels ordered during the 1960s, the Tarawa class LHAs were to combine in a single hull capabilities which had previously required a number of separate specialist types — the LPH, the LSD, LPD, the LCC and the LKA (see following entries). The result is a truly massive ship with more than twice the displacement of any previous amphibious unit and with dimensions approaching those of a conventional aircraft carrier. Nine ships were originally projected, to be constructed by means of advanced modular techniques at the same Litton/Ingalls yard that built the Spruance class destroyers. In 1971, however, with the Vietnam War drawing to a close, the order was reduced to five, resulting in some financial penalties.

The increase in size of these ships is a direct consequence of the need to provide a helicopter hangar *and* a docking-well. The hangar is located directly above the docking-well; both are 268ft in length and 78ft wide (81.6 × 23.7m), and the hangar has a 20ft (6.5m) overhead to enable the latest heavy-lift helicopters to be accommodated. In order to maximise internal capacity the ship's sides are vertical for two-thirds of its length. Hangar capacity is greater than that of the Iwo Jima class, and all the helicopters can be struck down if necessary. There is a deck-edge lift to port, and a larger centreline lift set into the stern.

Below: *Tarawa* (LHA 1) was the first of a series of designs of multi-rôle amphibious assault ships to be built during the 1970s.

The latter can handle the CH-53E Super Stallion heavy-lift helicopter.

From the late 1970s the Pacific-based ships began to operate Marine AV-8A Harriers and had their flight decks marked out accordingly. *Nassau* (LHA4) subsequently embarked 20 AV-8As to provide ground support for an amphibious exercise off northern Norway in 1981. The success of these trials influenced the design of the Wasp (LHD-1) class.

The docking-well can accommodate four of the big LCUs, which can each lift three M-48 or M-60 tanks, or 150 tons of cargo. Two LCM-6 landing-craft, which can each carry 80 troops or 34 tons of cargo, are stowed immediately abaft of the island and are handled by a large crane. The docking-well is divided into two by a central support structure incorporating a conveyor belt, which runs forward onto the vehicle decks. The conveyor belt is served by a group of three cargo elevators at its forward end, and by a further two elevators in the docking-well area. The elevators bring supplies for the landing force, stored in pallets each weighing approximately one ton, up from the cargo holds deep in the ship. The pallets are transferred to the landing-craft by one of 11 monorail cars which work overhead in the welldeck area. The after pair of elevators can also lift pallets directly to the hangar deck, where they are loaded onto transporters. An angled ramp leads from the hangar deck to the forward end of the island, enabling the transfer of pallets to the flight deck for loading onto the helicopters.

Forward of the docking-well are the vehicle decks, interconnected by a series of ramps and able to accommodate some 200 vehicles. Tanks, artillery and trucks are generally stowed at the forward end, and up to 40 LVTP-7 amphibious personnel carriers, each with a capacity of 25 troops, can be accommodated. Eight LVTPs can be launched from the welldeck simultaneously with the four big landing craft.

Above: *Saipan* (LHA 2) and *Nashville* (LPD 13) take on stores from the combat stores ship *Mars* (AFS 1).

Below: *Tarawa* off Hawaii. The after section of the vertically-sided hull houses the floodable docking well measuring 268ft in length by 78ft.

Above: *Nassau* (LPD 4) in the Gulf; the threat of a Marine landing served to throw the Iraqi forces in Kuwait City off balance.

Below: UH-1 Iroquois and AH-1 Sea Cobra helicopters, and AV-8 Harrier VTOL aircraft aboard *Nassau*, ever ready for an assault.

Above the vehicle decks is the accommodation deck, with berths for some 2,000 troops in addition to the 900 crew. At the forward end there is a combined acclimatisation room/gymnasium, in which humidity and temperature can be controlled to simulate the climate in which the troops will be operating. At the after end there is a large, well equipped hospital, which can if necessary expand into accommodation spaces. Separate personnel elevators serve the hospital and the accommodation area, enabling rapid transfers to and from the flight deck.

The large block superstructure houses extensive command facilities, with accommodation for both the Commander Amphibious Task Group (CATG) and the Landing Force Commander (LFC) and their respective staffs. To enable these officers to exercise full tactical control over amphibious operations the LHAs are provided with a computer-based Integrated Tactical Amphibious Warfare. Data System (ITAWDS), which keeps track of the position of troops, helicopters, vehicles, landing-craft and cargo after they leave the ship. The system also tracks the position of designated targets ashore, and aims and fires the ship's armament. Initially three 5in Mk 45 guns were provided for fire support of the troops ashore, together with two BPDMS Mk 25 missile launchers for self-defence. The latter have now been replaced by Mk 15 Phalanx CIWS, and the after gun mounting has been replaced by a control antenna for a drone reconnaissance aircraft.

The versatility of the LHAs enables them to combine with any of the other amphibious types in the US Navy inventory. A typical PhibRon deployment would combine an LHA with an LPD and one/two LSTs. The only major limitation of the design appears to be the inability to accommodate more than one of the new air-cushion landing-craft (AALC) because of the layout of the docking-well.

Iwo Jima

Completed:	1961-70.
Names:	LPH 2 *Iwo Jima*; LPH 3 *Okinawa*; LPH 7 *Guadalcanal*; LPH 9 *Guam*; LPH 10 *Tripoli*; LPH 11 *New Orleans*; LPH 12 *Inchon*.
Displacement:	11,000t light; 17,515-18,300t full load.
Dimensions:	Length 602ft oa (184m); beam 84ft wl (25.5m); 104ft flight deck (32m); draught 26ft (8m).
Propulsion:	One-shaft geared steam turbine; 22,000shp = 20kts.
Armament:	Two BPDS launchers Mk 25 (2 × 8, not in LPH 3); four 3in (76mm) Mk 33 guns (2 × 2); two Mk 15 Phalanx CIWS.
Aircraft:	Four CH-53D Sea Stallion; 20 CH-46D/E Sea Knight; four AH-IT/W Sea Cobra; four UH-IN Iroquois.
Troops:	1,900.
Sensors:	*Surveillance*: SPS-40, SPS-10.
	Fire-Control: Two Mk 115 (not in LPH-3).

The US Marine Corps had initiated experiments in helicopter assault techniques as early as 1948, and in 1955 the former escort carrier *Thetis Bay* underwent a major conversion to test the "vertical envelopment" concept. Two years later the escort carrier *Block Island* was taken in hand for a similar conversion, but this was halted as an economy measure. The concept proved such a success, however, that the Navy embarked on a programme of new purpose-built helicopter carriers, which became the Iwo Jima class. As an interim measure three Essex class carriers were modified for helicopter operations and reclassified as amphibious assault ships. These and the converted escort carriers took the "missing" LPH numbers in the series until their demise in the late 1960s.

As the ships of the Iwo Jima class were amphibious — not fleet — units, many of the refinements associated with first-line vessels were dispensed with in the interests of economy. The design was based on a mercantile hull with a one-shaft propulsion system capable of a sustained 20 knots. A large central box hangar was adopted with 20ft (6.5m) clearance, a capacity of about 20 helicopters, and with deck-edge lifts disposed *en echelon* at either end. The lifts, 50ft × 34ft (15.2m × 10.4m) and with a capacity of 22tons, can be folded

Below: *Inchon* (LPH 12) with a deckload of CH-46 Sea Knight and CH-53 Sea Stallion assault helicopters. AV-8s can also operate from her.

upwards to close the hangar openings. Fore and aft of the hangar there is accommodation for a Marine battalion, and the ships have a well equipped hospital containing 300 beds.

The flight deck is marked out with five helo spots along the port side and two to starboard. Helicopter assault operations are directed from a specialised Command Center housed in the island. The radar outfit is austere: air search and aircraft control antennae are fitted but these ships do not have the large 3-D antennae of the first-line carriers.

As completed, the Iwo Jima class had two twin 3in (76mm) mountings at the forward end of the island and two further mountings just below the after end of the flight deck. Between 1970 and 1974 the after port mounting and the first of the two forward mountings were replaced by BPDMS launchers. All seven ships have now been fitted with two Mk 15 Phalanx CIWS; in *Okinawa* (LPH 3) these replace the Mk 25 BPDMS launchers, whereas in other units they are located on hull sponsons to port and to starboard.

Below: *Iwo Jima* (LPH 2) and her sisters now have two Phalanx CIWS on sponsons in addition to their original Sea Sparrow surface-to-air missile systems, giving good protective cover against attack.

Below: Note the arrangement of the deck-edge lifts in this overhead view of *Guadalcanal* (LPH 7). The broad line marks out the take-off run for the AV-8 Harrier, operable following capability modifications.

From 1972 until 1974 *Guam* (LPH 9) was trials ship for the Sea Control Ship (SCS) concept, in which role she operated a mix of ASW helicopters and Marine AV-8A Harriers. An Air-Surface Classification and Analysis Center (ASCAC) was installed, and a carrier-controlled approach (CCA) radar fitted. Although operations with the Harrier were particularly successful and have been continued on a routine basis in the larger Tarawa class LHAs, the Sea Control Ship did not find favour with the US Navy, and *Guam* has since reverted to her assault ship role.

The Iwo Jima class generally operates in conjunction with ships of the LPD, LSD and LST types. Although *Inchon*, the last ship built, carries two LCVPs, the LPHs have no significant ability to land troops, equipment and supplies by any means other than by helicopter. The troops are therefore lightly equipped and would be employed as an advance echelon, landing behind the enemy's shore defences and relying on a follow-up frontal assault staged by more heavily equipped units brought ashore by landing-craft from the other vessels in the supporting squadron.

Below: *Tripoli* **(LPH 10) in the Gulf. She sustained severe damage when she struck a mine while operating off the Kuwaiti coast in February 1991, an occasion when airborne minesweeping was to no avail.**

LPD
Austin

Completed:	1965-71.
Names:	LPD 4 *Austin*; LPD 5 *Ogden*; LPD 6 *Duluth*;
	LPD 7 *Cleveland*; LPD 8 *Dubuque*; LPD 9 *Denver*;
	LPD 10 *Juneau*; LPD 12 *Shreveport*;
	LPD 13 *Nashville*; LPD 14 *Trenton*; LPD 15 *Ponce*.
Displacement:	11,050t light; 17,595t full load.
Dimensions:	Length 570ft oa (173.4m); beam 84ft (25.6m); draught 23ft (7m).
Armament:	Four 3in (76mm) Mk 33 guns (2 × 2); two Mk 15 Phalanx CIWS.
Aircraft:	Up to six CH-46D (see notes).
Troops:	840-930
Landing-craft:	One LCU, three LCM-6.
Sensors:	*Surveillance*: SPS-40, SPS-10.

The Austin class is a development of the Raleigh class, which instituted the LPD concept. The major modification was the insertion of a 50ft (15.2m) hull section forward of the docking-well. This resulted in a significant increase in vehicle space and cargo capacity (3,900 tons compared to only 2,000 tons for the Raleigh class). The additional length available for flying operations enabled a large telescopic hangar to be worked in immediately abaft the superstructure. Up to six CH-46 Sea Knight or CH-53 Sea Stallion troop-carrying helicopters can be carried for brief periods, but the hangar can accommodate only a single utility helicopter.

Troop accommodation and docking-well capacity are identical to those of *Raleigh*, except that LPD 7-13 are configured as amphibious squadron (PhibRon) flagships and can accommodate only 840 troops. The latter ships can be outwardly distinguished by their extra bridge level.

Two of the original four twin 3in (76mm) mountings, together with all fire-control radars, were removed in the late 1970s. The five units serving with the Atlantic Fleet had all received two Mk 15 Phalanx CIWS by the late 1980s.

In 1980 *Coronado* (LPD 11) was redesignated AGF 11 and served temporarily as Command Ship for the Middle East Force; she became flagship of the US Third Fleet in 1986.

Above: *Shreveport* (LPD-12), with Mk 15 Phalanx CIWS port and starboard. Two of the original four 3in gun mountings have been retained, but the fire-control system has been removed.

Left: A stern view of *Shreveport*, showing the gate for the docking well. The telescopic hangar can be seen just forward of the two CH-53 Sea Stallion assault helicopters. Sea Cobras are often carried too.

LPD
Raleigh

Completed:	1962-63.
Names:	LPD 1 *Raleigh*; LPD 2 *Vancouver*.
Displacement:	8,480t light; 14,865t full load.
Dimensions:	Length 522ft oa (159m); beam 84ft (25.6m); draught 22ft (6.7m).
Propulsion:	Two-shaft geared steam turbines; 24,000shp = 20kts.
Armament:	Six 3in (76mm) Mk 33 (3 × 2); two Mk 15 Phalanx CIWS.
Troops:	930.
Landing-craft:	One LCU, three LCM-6.
Sensors:	*Surveillance*: SPS-40, SPS-10.

Raleigh was the prototype of a new amphibious class employing the "balanced load" concept. Previous amphibious task forces carried troops in Attack Transports (APA), cargo in Attack Cargo Ships (AKA), and landing craft and tanks in Dock Landing Ships (LSD). The basic principle of the "balanced force" concept is that these three capabilities are combined in a single hull. The docking-well in the

Raleigh class therefore occupies only the after part of the ship, while forward of the well there are vehicle decks, cargo holds and substantial troop accommodation decks. The well itself measures 168ft × 50ft (51m × 15m) — less than half the length of the docking-well in the most modern LSDs — and is served overhead by six monorail cars, which load cargo into the awaiting landing-craft. The docking-well can accommodate one LCU and three LCM-6s, or four LCM-8s. Two further LCM-6s and four LCPLs are carried at the after end of the superstructure, and are handled by a large crane.

The docking-well is covered by a helicopter landing platform, which can receive up to six CH-46 Sea Knight troop-carrying helicopters. The Raleigh class, unlike the later Austins, has no hangar or maintenance facilities and therefore relies on an accompanying LPH or LHA to provide helicopters for vertical assault operations. The flight deck can also be used as additional vehicle space, and there are ramps connecting the flight deck, the vehicle decks and the docking-well.

The port forward twin Mk 33 gun mounting and all fire-control systems were removed in 1977-78. Two Mk 15 Phalanx CIWS have now been fitted.

A third ship of the class, *La Salle*, serves as a Command Ship numbered AGF 3 for the US Middle East Force.

Below: *Vancouver* **(LPD 2) and her sister do not have the telescopic helicopter hangar fitted to later LPDs. They will serve until the late 1990s.**

Whidbey Island

Completed:	1985 onwards.
Names:	LSD 41 *Whidbey Island*; LSD 42 *Germantown*; LSD 43 *Fort McHenry*; LSD 44 *Gunston Hall*; LSD 45 *Comstock*; LSD 46 *Tortuga*; LSD 47 *Rushmore*; LSD 48 *Ashland*; LSD 49 *Harpers Ferry* †; LSD 50 *Cartertown*†; LSD 51-53‡. (†building ‡projected.)
Displacement:	11,855t light; 15,745t full load.
Dimensions:	Length 609ft oa (185.8m); beam 84ft (25.6m); draught 20ft (6m).
Propulsion:	Two-shaft diesel; four Colt-Pielstick 16-cyl.; 34,000shp = 22kts.
Armament:	Two Mk 15 Phalanx CIWS; two 20mm Mk 67 AA.
Troops:	560.
Landing-craft:	Four LCAC.
Sensors:	*Surveillance*: SPS-49, SPS-67.

The LSD 41 design was prepared in the mid-1970s as a replacement for the eight ships of the Thomaston class. It was the first US Navy amphibious vessel to be designed specifically to operate the air-cushion LCAC, which can carry an MBT or 60 tons of cargo to the beach at a speed of 40kts. Four can be accommodated in the docking-well, which is identical in width to that of the Anchorage class but 10ft (3m) longer. An optical guidance system assists LCAC entry to the well-deck.

The capacious helicopter deck, which measures 212ft × 83ft (65m × 25m), is strong enough to receive the Marine CH-53E Super Stallion cargo-carrying helicopter, for which there are two operating spots. It extends to the stern, and is raised on stanchions above the docking well to allow all-round ventilation for the gas-turbines of the LCAC. A single LCVP carried on deck is handled by a 60-ton crane, and there are two LCPL handled by a 20-ton crane.

The Whidbey Island class has been built using modular construction techniques, and differs from previous types in adopting diesel propulsion in place of steam turbines. The diesel engines are installed as two independent units, and have proved very economical.

LSD 44 onwards have an NBC close-down system. LSD 49 onwards belong to a separate sub-group (the Harpers Ferry class). These ships will have a shorter-well-deck capable of accommodating only two LCAC or 10 LCM (6). Vehicle space will be virtually unchanged, but cargo capacity will be 40,000ft³ (1,133m³) as compared with only 5,000ft³ (149m³) for LSD 41-48.

Above: *Comstock* (LSD 45), one of a new class of LSDs designed to operate four air-cushion LCACs. The programme's future is uncertain.

Below: The LCAC is significantly faster than conventional landing craft; it can carry 60 tons of cargo at 40 knots.

Anchorage

Completed:	1969-72.
Names:	LSD 36 *Anchorage*; LSD 37 *Portland*; LSD 38 *Pensacola*; LSD 39 *Mount Vernon*; LSD 40 *Fort Fisher*.
Displacement:	8,600t light; 13,700t full load.
Dimensions:	Length 553ft (168.7m); beam 84ft (25.6m); draught 19ft (5.6m).
Propulsion:	Two-shaft geared steam turbines; 24,000shp — 20kts.
Armament:	Six 3in (76mm) Mk 33 (3 × 2).
Troops:	375.
Landing-craft:	Three LCU, one LCM-6.
Sensors:	*Surveillance*: SPS-40, SPS-10.

The five dock landing ships of the Anchorage class were among the last units to be completed in the large amphibious ship programme of the 1960s. In spite of the advent of the LPD with its "balanced load" concept, there was still a requirement for LSDs to carry additional landing-craft to the assault area. The Anchorage class was therefore built to replace the ageing war-built vessels,

which had inadequate speed for the new PhibRons. It is a development of the Thomaston class (now in reserve).

The docking-well measures 430ft by 50ft (131m × 15.2m) — an increase of 30ft (9m) in length over the Thomastons — and can accommodate three of the big LCUs or nine LCM-8s, with an alternative loading of 50 LVTP-7s. There is space on deck for a single LCM-6, and an LCPL and an LCVP are carried on davits. There are vehicle decks above the docking-well amidships, served by two 50-ton cranes. The Anchorage class was designed to transport up to 30 helicopters, and there is a removable flight deck aft for heavy-lift cargo helicopters.

The sensor outfit and armament are on a par with the contemporary LPDs of the Austin class (which are described on pages 118-119). Four twin 3in (76mm) mountings were originally fitted, but one was removed, together with all fire-control radars, in the late 1970s. Two Mk 15 Phalanx CIWS were fitted in the two Atlantic-based ships during the late 1980s.

The Anchorage class is due to be replaced by a variant of the Whidbey Island (LSD 54-59) class towards the end of the decade.

Below: *Anchorage* (LSD 36) and her sisters can accommodate three large utility landing craft (LCU) or nine LCM-8s in their 430ft docking wells. Note the two Phalanx and the 50-ton capacity crane.

Newport

Completed: 1969-72.

Names: LST 1179 *Newport*; LST 1180 *Maniwotoc*;
LST 1181 *Sumter*; LST 1182 *Fresno*; LST 1183 *Peoria*;
LST 1184 *Frederick*; LST 1185 *Schenectady*;
LST 1186 *Cayuga*; LST 1187 *Tuscaloosa*;
LST 1188 *Saginaw*; LST 1189 *San Bernadino*;
LST 1190 *Boulder*; LST 1191 *Racine*;
LST 1192 *Spartanburg County*; LST 1193 *Fairfax County*;
LST 1194 *La Moure County*; LST 1195 *Barbour County*;
LST 1196 *Harlan County*; LST 1197 *Barnstable County*;
LST 1198 *Bristol County*.

Displacement: 4,795t light; 8,450t full load.

Dimensions: Length 562ft oa (171m); beam 70ft (21m); draught 18ft (5m).

Propulsion: Two-shaft diesels; six GM (LST 1179-81)/Alco (others); 16,500bhp = 20kts.

Armament: Four 3in (76mm) Mk 33 (2 × 2); one Mk 15 Phalanx CIWS.

Sensors: *Surveillance*: SPS-10.

The twenty LSTs of the Newport class are larger and faster than the war-built vessels they replaced. In order to match the 20-knot speed of the other amphibious units built during the 1960s the traditional bow doors were suppressed in favour of a 112ft (34m) ramp which is lowered over the bows of the ship between twin fixed derrick arms. This arrangement also allowed for an increase in draught in line with the increase in displacement.

Below: A tank landing ship of the Newport class unloads vehicles via a bow ramp slung between its massive derrick arm "jaws".

There is a large integral flight deck aft for utility helicopters. Four pontoon causeway sections can be slung on either side of the flight deck for use in landing operations. Each can carry an MBT and they can be mated with the stern gate.

Below decks there is a total parking area of 19,000ft² (1,765m²) for a cargo capacity of 500 tons of vehicles. The forecastle is connected to the vehicle deck by a ramp and to the flight deck by a passageway through the superstructure. A through-hull bow thruster is provided to maintain the ship's position while unloading offshore.

Fire-control systems for the 3in Mk 33 guns were removed in 1977-78. Atlantic-based ships have received a single Mk 15 Phalanx CIWS, and it is still envisaged that both Mk 33 gun mountings will be replaced by Phalanx in all ships.

Below: LVTP-7 amphibious personnel carriers return to the *Newport* (LST 1179) during an exercise in the Atlantic Ocean.

Support Ships

Yellowstone & Samuel Gompers

Completed:	1967-83.
Names:	AD 37 *Samuel Gompers*; AD 38 *Puget Sound*; AD 41 *Yellowstone*; AD 42 *Acadia*; AD 43 *Cape Cod*; AD 44 *Shenandoah*.
Displacement:	(AD 37, 38) 13,600t light; 20,500t full load. (AD 41-44) 13,320t light; 20,225t full load.
Dimensions:	Length 644ft oa (196m); beam 85ft (26m); draught 23ft (7m).
Propulsion:	One-shaft geared steam turbines; 20,000shp = 18kts.
Armament:	Two 40mm Mk 19 grenade launchers; two/four 20mm AA (2/4 × 1).
Sensors:	*Surveillance*: SPS-10.

Samuel Gompers and *Puget Sound* were the navy's first destroyer tenders built to a postwar design. They are similar in size and general configuration to the contemporary SSBN tenders of the Simon Lake class, but were specifically fitted out to support surface combatants on forward deployment. They can furnish in-port service to six cruiser/destroyer types alongside simultaneously. The high-sided hull and the superstructures contain approximately 60 workshops to enable these ships to maintain and repair the latest equipment, including missile systems. ASW weapons, advanced communications and electronics and nuclear propulsion plants. There are two 30-ton kingpost cranes to handle heavier items such as propellers and machinery, and two 6-ton travelling cranes for smaller

Below: The two 30-ton kingpost cranes can handle propellers and machinery. This is *Yellowstone* (AD 41), successor to the Dixie class.

items of equipment. A hangar and platform were provided for DASH, but the hangar proved too small for manned helicopters and that on *Samuel Gompers* has been converted into a boat repair shop. A single 5in/38 cal. gun initially fitted forward of the bridge was removed in 1979.

The Yellowstone class is a follow-on design intended to replace the ageing tenders of the Dixie class. Improvements over the Gompers class include increased supply and stowage capacity, the fitting of heavier travelling cranes, the provision of two 50ft (15m) LCM workboats primarily designed for handling weapons, and a rationalised layout of workshops. There is also topside stowage at 01 deck level for spare gas turbines for the CG 47, DD 963, FFG 7 and PHM 1 types. Plans to fit Sea Sparrow forward of the bridge were abandoned. Both classes have the Navy Automated Communications System.

Above: *Samuel Gompers* (AD 37) was the first of a new generation of destroyer tenders. Introduced in the 1960s she is Pacific-based.

Emory S. Land/L.Y. Spear

Completed:	1970-81.
Names:	AS 36 *L.Y. Spear*; AS 37 *Dixon*; AS 39 *Emory S. Land*; As 40 *Frank Cable*; AS 41 *McKee*.
Displacement:	(AS 36, 37) 12,770t light; 23,495t full load (AS 39-41) 13,840t light; 22,650t full load.
Dimensions:	Length 644ft oa (196m); beam 85ft (26m); draught 25ft (7.7m).
Propulsion:	One-shaft geared steam turbines; 20,000shp = 18kts.
Armament:	Two 40mm Mk 19 grenade launchers (AS 39-41 only); four 20mm AA (4 × 1).
Sensors:	*Surveillance*: SPS-10.

Derived from the SSBN tenders of the Simon Lake class, *L.Y. Spear* and *Dixon* were the first submarine tenders to be designed to support SSNs, for which they provide repairs, spare parts, provisions, ordnance and medical facilities.

There are three Ship Alongside Service (SAS) stations supplied through four switchboards. Services supplied include compressed air, oxygen, nitrogen, 150lb (68kg) steam, oil, water and electrical power. A single 15-ton kingpost crane immediately forward of the funnel handles propellers and heavy machinery, and other items of equipment are handled by two 5-ton travelling cranes with a 55ft (17m) outreach, running on tracks which cover the entire midships section. There is a helicopter deck but no hangar or maintenance facilities. Single 5in/38 cal. guns initially fitted fore and aft were subsequently removed.

The Emory S. Land class is a follow-on design fitted specifically for the support of SSNs of the Los Angeles class. Two ships serve in the Atlantic, and *McKee* (AS 41) in the Pacific. Improvements over the Spear class include an increase in crane capacity — that of the kingpost crane has been doubled in order to handle the heavier machinery of the Los Angeles class — and an increase in generating power. There are 53 workshops and 16 magazines on 13 deck levels. Up to four submarines can be supported alongside simultaneously. During the 1980s *Dixon* (AS 37) was equipped to support Tomahawk cruise missiles.

Below: The submarine tender *Dixon* (AS 37) at the San Diego Submarine Support Facility. Two SSNs are moored alongside.

Simon Lake

Completed: 1964-65.
Names: AS 33 *Simon Lake*; AS 34 *Canopus*.
Displacement: 12,000 light; 21,090t full load.
Dimensions: Length 644ft oa (196m); beam 85ft (26m); draught 28ft (8.7m).
Propulsion: One-shaft geared steam turbines; 20,000shp = 18kts.
Armament: Four 3in (76mm) Mk 33 guns (2 × 2).
Sensors: *Surveillance*: SPS-10.

The two SSBN tenders of the Simon Lake class are larger than their immediate predecessors of the Hunley class and have a much improved layout. The funnel and machinery are well aft, leaving the midships section clear for cranage and services to support up to three submarines lying alongside. There is a full reactor support capability and facilities are provided for the handling, replacement and limited servicing of SLBMs. Sixteen missiles are stowed vertically amidships. Both ships were modified 1969-71 to enable them to handle the Poseidon C-3, and subsequently for the Trident C-4 missile. Two 30-ton cranes are fitted amidships, and there are four 5-ton travelling cranes. A helicopter platform is provided for VERTREP.

A third ship due for authorization in FY 65 was cancelled.

Below: The submarine tender *Simon Lake* (AS 33) off Hawaii. She and her sister *Canopus* now serve in the Atlantic, where they support the SSBNs of the Lafayette class. The two kingpost cranes can handle the Poseidon SLBM. *Simon Lake* can also manage Trident.

AS
Hunley

Completed:	1961-63.
Names:	AS 31 *Hunley*; AS 32 *Holland*.
Displacement:	11,000t light; 19,820t full load.
Dimensions:	Length 599ft oa (183m); beam 83ft (25m); draught 24ft (7m).
Propulsion:	One-shaft diesel-electric; six Fairbanks-Morse diesels; 15,000bhp = 19kts.
Armament:	Four 20mm (4 × 1).
Sensors:	*Surveillance*: SPS-10.

These were the first purpose-built SSBN tenders. They can supply services to three submarines alongside simultaneously and support a squadron of nine. There are 52 workshops and extensive stowage facilities, including vertical stowage for SLBMs. These were originally handled by a massive 32-ton hammerhead crane with athwartships travel, but this has since been replaced by two conventional kingpost cranes. There is a helicopter platform aft for VERTREP operations. Both ships were modified 1973-75 to enable them to handle the Poseidon C-3 missile.

It is unlikely that these two ships will survive the decomissioning of the remaining SSBNs armed with Poseidons.

Below: *Hunley* **(AS 31) was the first purpose-built tender for the Navy's Polaris submarines. Both ships were modified in the 1970s to enable them to handle Poseidon. They will probably pay off in the near future as the Poseidon-armed submarines are phased out.**

Replenishment Ships

AE
Kilauea

Completed: 1968-72.
Names: T-AE 26 *Kilauea*; AE 27 *Butte*; AE 28 *Santa Barbara*;
AE 29 *Mount Hood*; AE 33 *Shasta*; .
AE 34 *Mount Baker*; AE 35 *Kiska*.
Displacement: 9,240t light; 19,935t full load.
Dimensions: Length 564ft oa (172m); beam 81ft (24.7m); draught 28ft
(8.5m).
Propulsion: One-shaft geared steam turbine; 22,000shp = 20kts.
Armament: Four 3in (76mm) Mk 33 (2 × 2); two Mk 15 Phalanx
CIWS.
Helicopters: Two UH-46 Sea Knight.
Sensors: *Surveillance*: SPS-10.

The eight ammunition ships of the Kilauea class belong to the generation of underway replenishment vessels constructed during the 1960s. They are similar in size to the combat stores ships of the Mars class, but specialise in the transfer of missiles and other munitions. Improvements in layout include the merging of the bridge and hangar structures into a single block, leaving the entire forward and midships areas clear for transfer operations. The central section of the hull is a deck higher than that of the Mars class, providing the additional internal

Below: The ammunition ships of the Kilauea class carry two UH-46 helicopters for vertical replenishment (VERTREP).

volume for the stowage of missiles. There are six pairs of transfer stations and fin stabilisers ensure a steady platform for the transfer of the ships' delicate cargo.

The twin hangars can accommodate two UH-46 VERTREP helicopters. All ships initially had two twin 3in (76mm) mounts and Mk 56 GFCS on the hangar roof but these were removed in the late 1970s. Two Phalanx CIWS are currently being fitted to the ships.

Kilauea (formerly AE 26) was disarmed and transferred to the Military Sealift Command in 1980. Other units have had some of their solid stores transfer stations de-activated in order to reduce crew size.

Above: *Butte* **(AE 27) during Exercise "Distant Drum". The capacious hold amidships can accommodate missiles up to 6,500 tons in total.**

AE
Suribachi

Completed:	1956-59.
Names:	AE 21 *Suribachi*; AE 22 *Mauna Kea*; AE 23 *Nitro*; AE 24 *Pyro*; AE 25 *Haleakala*;
Displacement:	10,000t light; 17,000t full load.
Dimensions:	Length 512ft oa (156m); beam 72ft (22m); draught 29ft (8.8m).
Propulsion:	One-shaft geared steam turbine; 16,000shp = 20.6kts.
Armament:	Four 3in (76mm) Mk 33 guns (2 × 2).
Sensors:	SPS-10.

Built from the keel up as Navy ships, the Suribachi class were among the first specialised underway replenishment vessels built postwar. As completed, they were equipped with conventional mercantile kingposts and booms for the transfer of bombs and other munitions. Elevators were provided for the internal handling of ammunition and explosives, and the design incorporated air conditioning and the latest methods of stowage. A sixth ship was to have been built under the FY 1959 Program but was cancelled.

Soon after completion, all five ships underwent an extensive modernisation to enable them to handle the new surface-to-air missiles. Three holds were rigged for the stowage of missiles up to the size of Talos, and fully mechanised handling facilities were provided to move the missiles to the transfer stations.

Below: *Suribachi* (AE 21) and her sisters were refitted with Fast Automatic Shuttle Transfer (FAST) stations during the 1960s.

The Fast Automatic Shuttle Transfer (FAST) system pioneered by the combat stores ships of the Mars class was installed, resulting in safer missile handling and reduced transfer times. The Suribachi class now has three kingposts, the first and third of which have constant-tension transfer stations on either side.

As completed, these ships had two twin 3in Mk 33 guns on the forecastle and a similar arrangement aft. Mk 56 and Mk 63 GFCS were provided. When the ships underwent modernisation in the mid-1960s, the after mountings and the fire-control systems were removed and a large flight deck for VERTREP helicopters was fitted above the stern. *Pyro* (AE 24) was transferred to the NRF in 1980, but was re-activated in 1982.

Below: The Suribachi class now have a large platform for VERTREP helicopters above the stern. They will serve for some years.

AFS

Mars

Completed:	1963-70.
Names:	AFS-1 *Mars*; AFS 2 *Sylvania*; AFS 3 *Niagara Falls*; AFS 4 *White Plains*; AFS 5 *Concord*; AFS 6 *San Diego*; AFS 7 *San Jose*.
Displacement:	9,400t light; 16,070t full load.
Dimensions:	Length 581ft oa (177m); beam 79ft (24m); draught 24ft (7.3m).
Propulsion:	One-shaft geared steam turbine; 22,000shp = 20kts.
Armament:	Four 3in (76mm) Mk 33 guns (2 × 2); two Mk 15 Phalanx CIWS.
Helicopters:	Two UH-46 Sea Knight;
Sensors:	*Surveillance*: SPS-10.

The seven combat stores ships of the Mars class were the first of a new generation of under-way replenishment vessels completed during the 1960s to support carrier task force deployments. They combine the functions of store ships (AF), stores-issue ships (AKS), and aviation store ships (AVS). Unlike the contemporary AOEs of the Sacramento class, however, they carry no fuel oil or other liquid cargo.

They were the first ships to incorporate the Fast Automatic Shuttle Transfer system (FAST), which revolutionised the handling of stores and munitions. Four "M" frames replace the conventional kingposts and booms of earlier vessels and these have automatic tensioning devices to keep the transfer lines taut while replenishing. Cargo capacity is 7,000 tons in five cargo holds. Computers provide up-to-the-minute data on stock status, with the data displayed on closed-circuit television (CCTV). The propulsion system is also fully automated and can be controlled from the bridge to ensure quick response during transfer operations. The ships normally steam on only two boilers, with the third shut down for routine maintenance.

Twin helicopter hangars are provided for VERTREP helicopters, enabling the ships to undertake vertical replenishment operations within a task force spread over a wide area.

As completed, the Mars class had four twin 3in (76mm) mounts and the Mk 56 GFCS. Two of the twin mounts and the fire-control system were removed in the late 1970s and two Mk 15 Phalanx CIWS are being fitted currently.

Above: *Niagara Falls* **(AFS 3) in the Gulf. These ships, like most today, have onboard helicopters for VERTREP operations.**

Below: The combat stores ships of the Mars class were the first to be fitted with the FAST stores transfer system.

AO
Cimarron

Completed: 1981-83.
Names: AO 177 *Cimarron*; AO 178 *Monongahela*;
AO 179 *Merrimack*; AO 180 *Willamette*; T-AO 186 *Platte*.
Displacement: 37,865 full load.
Dimensions: Length 708ft oa (216m); beam 83ft (25m); draught 35ft (10m).
Propulsion: One-shaft geared steam turbine; 24,000shp = 20kts.
Armament: Two Phalanx CIWS.
Sensors: *Surveillance*: SPS-55/10B.

The first fleet oilers to be completed for the US Navy since the mid-1950s, the Cimarron class were "sized" to provide two complete refuellings of a fossil-fuelled carrier together with its six/eight escorts. With a full load displacement of 27,500 tons and a length overall of 591ft (180.3m), they had a total capacity of 72,000 barrels of fuel oil, plus 48,000 barrels of JP-5 gas-turbine fuel. As completed, there were four constant-tension replenishment stations to port and three to starboard.

These ships have a distinctive elliptical underwater bow for improved seakeeping. Underway replenishment can be performed at a constant 15 knots, and there is a large platform aft for VERTREP helicopters. Unlike earlier AOs, they have a single superstructure block aft incorporating the bridge. Originally it was envisaged that they would have a crew of only 135, but this was increased to 181 in order to provide sufficient personnel to carry out maintenance on prolonged deployments.

During the late 1980s all five ships were taken in hand for "jumboizing" at the Avondale Shipyard where they were originally built. The hulls are being cut in two, and a 107ft (35m) section inserted amidships. Following modification fuel oil/JP-5 will be increased to 183,000 barrels, and dry stores capacity will be doubled, enabling munitions and a significant quantity of refrigerated stores to be carried. A new-design propeller and rudder are being fitted, underway transfer capabilities will be enhanced, and accommodations for the crew will increase to 235 berths. A full electronic warfare (EW) suite, comprising SLQ-32(V)1 ECM and Mk 36 Super RBOC chaff launchers, will be installed.

Below: _Cimarron_ (AO 177) as built. These ships are now being "jumboized"; an additional 107ft section will be inserted amidships to increase liquid cargo capacity from 130,000 barrels to 183,000 barrels. This programme should be completed in September 1992.

AOE
Supply

Completed:	1992 onwards.
Names:	AOE 6 *Supply*; AOE 7 *Rainier* †; AOE 8 *Arctic* †; AOE 9 . . . ‡ (†building ‡projected).
Displacement:	19,700t light; 48,800t full load.
Dimensions:	Length 755ft oa (230m); beam 107ft (32.6m); draught 39ft (12m).
Propulsion:	COGAG: four LM2500 gas turbines; 100,000shp = 26kts.
Armament:	One Sea Sparrow launcher Mk 29 (1 × 8); two Mk 15 Phalanx CIWS; two 25mm Mk 88 Bushmaster AA.
Helicopters:	Three UH-46 Sea Knight.
Sensors:	*Surveillance*: SPS-67.
	Fire-Control: Mk 91.

This class is a modification of the AOE 1 Sacramento class (q.v.), with new transfer gear and superior protective systems. The new "Standard Navy" UNREP suite devised for these ships is currently being trialled aboard *Camden* (AOE 2); it features new winches, rams, ram-tensioners and control booths. Liquid cargo capacity is 156,000 barrels, and 2,450 tons of dry stores can be carried, including 1,800 tons of munitions and 400 tons of refrigerated stores.

The Mk 29 launcher for Sea Sparrow is located forward of the bridge, and the Mk 15 Phalanxs are disposed *en echelon* fore and aft. The Supply class will be fitted from the outset with Mk 23 TAS and SLQ-32(V) 3 electronic counter-measures, together with four Mk 36 Super RBOC chaff launchers.

The 100,000shp required to power these ships at their maximum speed of 26 knots is provided by four LM2500 gas turbines, which power two six-bladed fixed-pitch propellers via a Franco Tosi-type clutch/gear box. The adoption of gas turbines in preference to geared steam turbines has resulted in an unusual silhouette, with two funnels in line atop a long after superstructure block.

Fifteen ships of this class were initially projected, in order to provide one AOE for each of 15 carrier battle groups. However, with the projected cuts in the number of battle groups, the AOE programme was reduced first to 11 ships and subsequently to only four, the last to be authorised under FY 1992. A provisional programme for a follow-on class of 16 AOE(V) combat support ships, intended to replace all existing AE, AFS, and AOR-type vessels with a uniform-design fuel and solid-stores carrier is still under consideration.

Above: The launch of the second ship, *Rainier* (AOE 7), at the San Diego shipyard of National Steel. Only four may now be built.

Below: The design of the Supply is based on that of *Sacramento* (AOE 1), but with gas turbine propulsion instead of steam.

Sacramento

Completed:	1964-70.
Names:	AOE 1 *Sacramento*; AOE 2 *Camden*; AOE 3 *Seattle*; AOE 4 *Detroit*.
Displacement:	18,700t light; 53,600t full load.
Dimensions:	Length 792ft oa (241m); beam 108ft (33m); draught 38ft (11.6m).
Propulsion:	Two-shaft geared steam turbines; 106,000shp = 26kts.
Armament:	One NATO Sea Sparrow launcher Mk 29 (1 × 8); two Mk 15 Phalanx CIWS.
Helicopters:	Two UH-46 Sea Knight.
Sensors:	*Surveillance*: SPS-40 (AOE 1/2), SPS-10.
	Fire-Control: Mk 91.

The world's largest under-way replenishment vessels, the fast combat support ships of the Sacramento class are designed to supply a carrier battle group with all its basic needs. They combine the functions of fleet oilers (AO), ammunition ships (AE), stores ships (AF) and cargo ships (AK). They have exceptionally high speed for their type to enable them to keep pace with fleet units. The machinery installed in *Sacramento* and *Camden* is from the cancelled battleship *Kentucky*, that in *Seattle* and *Detroit* is from *Illinois*.

Cargo capacity is 177,000 barrels of fuel oil, 2,150 tons of munitions and 750 tons of provisions. The Sacramento class was one of the first two designs to employ the FAST automatic transfer system. There are four refuelling stations to port and two to starboard — an arrangement which reflects their primary mission in support of the carriers — and there are three constant-tension transfer stations for dry stores to port and four to starboard. Aft there is a large helicopter deck with a three-bay hangar for VERTREP helicopters.

As completed, these ships each had four twin 3in (76mm) mounts, together with Mk 56 GFCS. The forward pair of mountings and the fire-control systems were removed in the mid-1970s and were subsequently replaced by a Sea Sparrow launcher with twin Mk 91 fire-control systems side by side atop the bridge. Two Mk 15 Phalanx CIWS were fitted in place of the after pair of 3in mountings during the late 1980s, together with Mk 23 TAS and SLQ-32(V)3 ECM.

The Sacramento class proved very expensive, and a fifth ship planned for FY 1968 was not built. Instead the smaller and less costly Wichita class AOR was developed as an alternative. The requirement for a twelfth AOE/AOR-type vessel to support a twelfth carrier battle group remained, however, and a fifth AOE was planned for the FY 1980 programme. Authorisation of this ship was further delayed while the US Navy re-assessed future needs. It eventually became the first of a new class (see AOE 6 *Supply*).

Below: The fast combat support ship *Camden* (AOE 2). Built to accompany the US Navy's carrier battle groups, these ships proved costly and were succeeded by the slower AOR.

AOR

Wichita

Completed:	1969-76.
Names:	AOR 1 *Wichita*; AOR 2 *Milwaukee*; AOR 3 *Kansas City* AOR 4 *Savannah*; AOR 5 *Wabash*; AOR 6 *Kalamazoo*; AOR 7 *Roanoke*.
Displacement:	13,000t light; 41,350t full load.
Dimensions:	Length 659ft oa (201m); beam 96ft (29.3m); draught 33ft (10m).
Propulsion:	Two-shaft geared steam turbines; 32,000shp = 20kts.
Armament:	One Sea Sparrow launcher Mk 29 (1 × 8); two Mk 15 Phalanx CIWS.
Helicopters:	Two UH-46 Sea Knight in AOR 2-3, 5, 7.
Sensors:	*Surveillance*: SPS-10.
	Fire-Control: Mk 91.

The Wichita class replenishment oilers, like the fast combat support ships of the Sacramento class, are designed for the support of the carrier battle groups. They are smaller vessels with much-reduced speed but have proved to be very successful ships. They carry a similar quantity of fuel oil to the larger AOEs but have only a limited capacity for provisions and munitions. This is reflected in their rig; there are four fuelling stations to port and three to starboard, but only two positions on either beam for the transfer of dry stores. Cargo capacity is 175,000 barrels of fuel, 600 tons of munitions and 575 tons of provisions.

AOR 1-6 were completed with two twin 3in (76mm) mountings above the flight deck aft, together with the Mk 56 GFCS. The last ship, however, was completed with a double helicopter hangar built around the funnel, and all other ships of the class subsequently received the same modification. The after guns were replaced by a Sea Sparrow SAM located at the after end of the hangar, with paired Mk 91 FC radars atop twin lattice masts forward of the funnel. Two Mk 15 Phalanx CIWS were installed forward of the bridge during the 1980s, and all except *Wichita* (AOR 1) have now received Mk 23 TAS. The ECM outfit is currently being upgraded to the standard of the Sacramento class (q.v.).

Above: The replenishment oiler *Milwaukee* (AOR 2). Although slower than the AOEs they have proved a very successful design.

Below: *Kansas City* (AOR 3) off Hawaii following duty in the Gulf. The Wichita class operates on only two boilers while maintaining the third.

Weapons and Sensors

Carrier-Borne Aircraft

F-14 Tomcat

In service: 1972.
Weight: 62,250lb (28,240kg) max.
Dimensions: Length 62ft (18.9m); wingspan 64ft (19.5m) max, 38ft (11.6m) swept; height 16ft (4.9m).

Fleet air-defence fighter with AWG-9 missile control system and six Phoenix/Sparrow/Sidewinder AAMs, plus one 20mm Vulcan gun. Standard variant is F-14A; F-14A Plus has new engine, and current-production F-14D has new avionics. Two 10/12-plane squadrons in all CVs (including a three-plane detachment with TARPS photo-recce pod).

Above: The F-14 Tomcat is the US Navy's premier fleet air defence fighter. It is seen landing armed with the Phoenix AAM.

Right: These state-of-the-art F/A-18 interceptor/attack aircraft are armed with HARM, Harpoon, Sparrow and Sidewinder missiles.

Below: The A-6E Intruder is for all-weather attack. This model is armed with HARM, a rocket pod and "iron bombs".

F/A-18 Hornet

In service: 1983.
Weight: 70,860lb (32,150kg) max.
Dimensions: Length 56ft (17.1m), wingspan 37ft (11.4m); height 15ft (4.7m).

Day interceptor/attack aircraft. Weapon load of four Sparrow, two Sidewinder AAMs, or 13,000lb (5,900kg) conventional/nuclear ordnance; APG-65 radar. F/A-18A now superseded by F/A-18C, with AMRAAM capability and improved EW suite. Two 10/12-plane squadrons in all CVs.

A-6 Intruder

In service: 1970 (A-6E).
Weight: 60,400lb (27,400kg).
Dimensions: Length 55ft (16.7m); wingspan 53ft (16.2m); height 16ft (4.9m).

All-weather/night attack aircraft. Standard A-6E variant can carry 18,000lb (8,170kg) of ordnance, including Harpoon, HARM, Maverick, Walleye plus Sidewinder AAMs. All have TRAM (Target Recognition Attack Multisensor); some have been re-engined/re-winged. KA-6D is tanker variant. One/two 10-plane squadrons in all CVs.

The last new A-6E aircraft was delivered in 1989. Its projected successor, the advanced A-12, has been cancelled because of rising costs.

EA-6B Prowler

In service: 1971.
Weight: 60,400lb (27,400kg) max.
Dimensions: Length 59ft (18.1m); wingspan 53ft (16.2m); height 16ft (5m).

Electronic warfare variant of A-6 Intruder. Four-man crew, APS-130 radar, five ALQ-99F jammer pods beneath wings/fuselage, and HARM missile capability. New ADVCAP variant will have improved engines and avionics. One four/five-plane detachment in all CVs.

E-2C Hawkeye

In service: 1973.
Weight: 52,500lb (23,800kg).
Dimensions: Length 58ft (17.6m); wingspan 81ft (24.6m); height 18ft (5.6m).

Airborne Early Warning (AEW) aircraft. APS-125/139 UHF radar in 24ft (7.3m) diameter saucer-shaped radome. Can track 600-plus air/surface targets within 250nm (463km) radius and control 25 simultaneous intercepts. One four/five-plane detachment in all CVs.

Above: The EA-6B Prowler is an electronic counter-measures variant of the A-6 Intruder. About 120 are in service.

Below: The E-2C Hawkeye is used for long-range surveillance and air command/control above the carrier battle group.

S-3 Viking

In service: 1974.
Weight: 52,650lb (23,850kg).
Dimensions: Length 53ft (16.3m); wingspan 69ft (20.9m); height 23ft (6.9m).

ASW aircraft with APS-116 radar and onboard AYK-10 digital computer for data-processing. Can carry four Mk 46 torpedoes plus 3,000lb (1,360kg) other ordnance. Original S-3A variant being upgraded to S-3B with improved avionics. One eight/10-plane squadron in all CVs.

SH-60F Ocean Hawk

In service: 1989.
Weight: 21,900lb (9,950kg).
Dimensions: Length 50ft (15.24m) fuselage; height 17ft (5.2m).

Derived from SH-60B LAMPS III as replacement for SH-3 Sea King in the inner-zone anti-submarine role. Fitted with Bendix AQS-13F dipping sonar, and carries two Mk 46 torpedoes plus 25 sonobuoys; does not have the APS-124 surface search radar of the SH-60B. One six-aircraft detachment is based aboard all aircraft carriers.

Above: The S-3A Viking ASW aircraft has its own onboard data processing facilities served by AYK-10 computers.

Below: The SH-60F Ocean Hawk is replacing the SH-3 Sea King and there are plans for a 175-strong force.

Surveillance Radars

SPY-1
In service: 1983.
S-Band Aegis multi-function radar, providing long range surveillance, target-tracking and missile guidance. Four fixed electronically-scanned planar arrays employed to give 360 deg coverage. SPY-1A and SPY-1B models on CG 47, lightweight SPY-1D on DDG 51.

SPS-48
In service: 1965.
S-Band 3-D radar with 230nm (426km) range. Large square planar antenna with electronic frequency scanning. In all CVs, early CGs and DDG 993 class. Standard SPS-48C model has Automatic Detection and Tracking (ADT). Currently being superseded by SPS-48E model with twice the power.

SPS-49
In service: 1977.
L-Band long range air surveillance radar. Fitted from outset in FFG 7 and CG 47 classes, has replaced SPS-37/43 series in CVs and early CGs. SPS-49(V)1 in FFG 7, (V)2 used in NTU upgrades, (V)5 is current ADT variant.

SPS-40
In service: 1962.
UHF medium-range (150-180nm) air surveillance radar. Fitted in DD 963 and FF 1052 classes and some amphibious and support ships. SPS-40B is standard model, superseded by "C" and "D" variants.

SPS-55
In service: 1975.
X-Band surface surveillance radar. In DD 963, FFG 7, CG 47 classes.

SPS-10/67
In service: 1953.
C-Band surface surveillance radar. SPS-10F standard model in older ships. SPS-67(V)1 is solid-state replacement using same antenna. SPS-67(V)3 for DDG 51 class employs new nuclear-survivable antenna and has automatic target detection.

Above: The SPY-1A Aegis multi-function radar comprises four hexagonal arrays which give 360-degree coverage.

Above: Over the SPQ-9 and SPG-62 FC antennae can be seen the SPS-55 navigation radar.

Above: The SPS-48, with its distinctive square planar array, is the standard Navy 3-D radar.

Above: For two-dimensional air surveillance the US Navy employs the SPS-49 L-Band radar in its surface combatants.

Air-Defence Weapons

Standard SM-1 MR Missile (RIM-66B)

In service: 1970.
Dimensions: Length 14ft 8in (4.5m); diameter 1ft 1in (0.34m).
Range: 25nm (46km) max.
Fire-Control: SPG-51.

Single-stage missile with semi-active homing. Fired from single-arm Mk 13 launcher (40-round magazine). In CGN 36 and FFG 7 classes.

Standard SM-2 MR Missile (RIM-66C)

In service: 1983.
Dimensions: Length 15ft 5in (4.7m); diameter 1ft 1in (0.34m).
Range: 40nm (74km) max.
Fire-Control: SPG-51, SPG-62.

Single-stage missile with inertial reference, mid-course guidance, semi-active terminal homing, and improved ECCM. Fired from Mk 26 launcher (24/44-round magazine) or from Mk 41 VLS (61/29-round magazine). New SM-2 Aegis (Block IV) is boosted variant with length of 27ft 4in (8.3m) and range of 75-plus nm (139km).

Standard SM-2 ER Missile (RIM-67B)

In service: 1983.
Dimensions: Length 26ft 2in (7.98m); diameter 1ft 1in (0.34m) missile, 1ft 6in (0.46m) booster.
Range: 75-100nm (139-185km) max.
Fire-Control: SPG-55.

Extended-range variant of above with finned booster for CGs with Mk 10 twin-arm launcher (40/60/80-round magazine).

Sea Sparrow Missile (RIM-7H/M)

In service: 1977.
Dimensions: Length 12ft (3.65m); diameter 8in (0.2m).
Range: 8nm (15km) max.
Fire-Control: Mk 91.

Short-range missile for self-defence with continuous wave active homing. Development of Sparrow AAM with folding wings, fired from 8-round box launcher Mk 29 with manual reloading. In CVs, DD 963 class, some amphibious and support ships. Official US Navy designation: Improved Point Defense Missile System (IPDMS).

Below: A Standard SM-2 MR missile is fired from a Mk 26 twin-arm launcher. Other ships use the Mk 41 Vertical Launch System.

20mm/76 cal.Mk 15 Phalanx CIWS

In service: 1980.
Range: 1,600yds (1,450m).
Fire-Control: Mk 90.

Six-barrelled close-in weapon system (CIWS) with on-mount radar, designed to destroy SSMs. 3,000rpm. Three/four installations in CVs, one/two in surface combatants, amphibious and some support vessels.

Above: The Standard SM-2 ER missile is a boosted variant fired from the twin-arm Mk 10 launcher of older CGs. It mixes command and inertial guidance.

Above: Sea Sparrow is fired from an eight-cell box launcher. It equips most combatants not armed with an area defence system and has been exported widely.

Below: The Mk 15 Phalanx CIWS features a rapid-firing multi-barrel 20mm gun, some 3,000 rounds per minute, and an on-mount radar.

Anti-Submarine Warfare

SH-60B Seahawk (LAMPS III)

In service: 1984.
Weight: 20,800lb (9,435kg).
Dimensions: Length 50ft (15.24m) fuselage; height 17ft (5.2m).
Replacement for SH-2F/G Seasprite. Fitted with APS-124 search radar. All sensors display on control ship via data link. Carries two Mk 46 torpedoes plus 25 sonobuoys. Can provide over-the-horizon targeting for ship-launched SSMs. In CG 47, DD 963 and FFG 7 classes.

SH-2 Seasprite (LAMPS I)

In service: 1971.
Weight: 13,500lb (6,125kg).
Dimensions: Length 38ft 5in (11.7m) fuselage; height 15ft 4in (4.7m).
First US Navy manned ASW helicopter to serve aboard surface ships. Fitted with LN-66 search radar. Control exercised from ship via data link. Carries two Mk 46 torpedoes plus 15 sonobuoys. Standard version is SH-2F; current SH-2G variant has new engines and improved avionics. In CG 26, DDG 993, DD 963, FFG 7 and FF 1052 classes.

Above: An SH-60B Seahawk LAMPS III (Light Airborne Multi-Purpose System) helicopter flies over USS *South Carolina* (CGN 37).

Above: An SH-2F Seasprite in low-visibility colours. The new SH-2G model has improved engines, avionics and sensor processing.

ASROC (RUR-5A)

In service: 1961
Dimensions: Length 14ft 9in (4.5m); diameter 1ft 1in (0.34m).
Range: 10,000yds (9,100m).
Fire-Control: Mk 114 or Mk 116.

Anti-submarine rocket with ballistic trajectory fitted in all major surface units except those with Mk 41 VLS. Payload Mk 46 torpedo. Mk 16 eight-cell launcher with semi-automatic loading in CGN 36, FF 1052, automatic loading in DD 963. Carried in mixed magazines in ships with Mk 10 or Mk 26 launcher. Vertical-launch boosted variant which had been under development for Mk 41 VLS has now been cancelled.

Mk 46 Torpedo

In service: 1964
Dimensions: Length 8ft 6in (2.6m); diameter 12.75in (324mm).
Range: 12,000yds (11,000m) at 40kts.
Guidance: Passive/active homing.

Standard US Navy ship/air-launched ASW torpedo since mid-1960s. Fired from triple trainable or fixed single Mk 32 tubes. Current variant is Mod 5 NEARTIP which has been widely exported.

Mk 50 ALWT Torpedo (Barracuda)

In service: Early 1990s
Dimensions: Length 9ft 3in (2.8m); diameter 12.75in (324mm).
Range: Unknown.
Guidance: Passive/active homing.

Intended as counter to deep-diving submarines such as Soviet Alfa class. Can engage submarines down to 600m. Closed-cycle thermal propulsion for high speed. Was to have been payload for vertical-launch ASROC.

Above: An ASROC missile, armed with a Mk 46 torpedo, is launched from an eight-cell Mk 112 launcher. Note the blast effect.

Anti-Surface Warfare

Tomahawk Missile (BGM-109)

In service: 1983
Dimensions: Length 20ft 3in (6.2m); diameter 1ft 8in (0.52m).
Range: 675nm (1,251km) (TLAM); 250nm (463km) (TSAM).
Fire-Control: Active radar/anti-radiation homing.

Long range anti-submarine missile using Tercom-Aided Inertial Navigation System (TAINS) to locate land target, external guidance against surface ships. Fired from four-missile Mk 44 armoured box launchers or Mk 41 VLS aboard surface ships; submarine-launched missiles fired from torpedo tubes in special container. Strategic variant with 1,400nm (2,594km) range to be phased out in near future.

Harpoon Missile (RBM-84)

In service: 1977
Dimensions: Length 15ft (4.6m); diameter 1ft 1in (0.34m).
Range: 75-80nm/148km.
Fire-Control: Active radar homing.

Medium-range anti-ship missile. Fired from lightweight canisters fixed to quadruple ramps or from Mk 13/26 launcher magazines; fired from submarine torpedo tubes in special container. In virtually all surface combatants, LAMPS helicopters provide guidance beyond the horizon to enable proper and accurate targeting of objectives.

Above: A Tomahawk land attack missile (TALM) is fired at Baghdad from *Mississippi* (CGN 40) during the Gulf War.

5in/54 cal. Mk 45 (single)

In service: 1974
Range: 13nm (24km) max.
Fire-Control: SPG-60, SPQ-9A with Mk 86 GFCS.
Lightweight dual-purpose gun with modest performance (16/20rpm) but high reliability and low manning requirements. In all major surface combatants completed since mid-1970s.

5in/54 cal. Mk 42 (single)

In service: 1953
Range: 13nm (24km) max.
Fire-Control: SPG-53 with Mk 68 GFCS.
Designed as high-performance (40rpm) dual-purpose gun. Unreliability led to modifications; now only 20rpm. Older surface combatants.

76mm/62 cal. Mk 75 (single)

In service: 1977
Range: 10nm (19km) max.
Fire-Control: Mk 92.
Lightweight high-performance dual-purpose gun manufactured in the USA under licence from OTO Melara. Rate of fire is 85rpm. Mk 92/94 fire-control system is US Navy adaptation of Dutch HSA WM-20 track-while-scan radar. Only in FFG 7 and PHM at the time of writing.

Above: Harpoon missiles are generally housed in canisters.

Above: Missile firing from a Mk 41 vertical launch system (VLS).

Above: *Antietam* (CG 54) has 5in Mk 45 guns and Mk 41 VLS fore and aft, with canisters for Harpoon SSMs on the stern.

OTHER SUPER-VALUE MILITARY GUIDES IN THIS SERIES

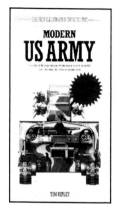

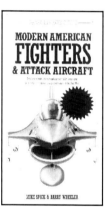

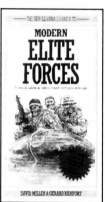

OTHER ILLUSTRATED MILITARY GUIDES AVAILABLE

Allied Fighters of World War II
Modern Tanks & Fighting Vehicles
Modern Rifles & Sub-Machine Guns
Modern Attack Aircraft
Weapons of the Elite Forces

★ Each title has 160 fact-filled pages
★ Each is colorfully illustrated with hundreds of action photographs and technical drawings
★ Each contains concisely presented data and accurate descriptions of major international weapons systems
★ Each title represents tremendous value for money